Heroine's
Journey
for
Filmmakers

The
Heroine's
Journey
for
Filmmakers

How to Create Female Characters that Females Relate To

DENISE ROSS, MIIS

ISBN: 978-1-7348895-0-5

Editor: Jessica Vineyard, Red Letter Editing, www.Redletterediting.com
Interior design and layout: Constellation Books Services

This book is dedicated to the four most amazing souls that I have ever known:

Matthew, Michele, Ali, and Ross.

You are the loves of my life and the truest forms of heroes and heroines.

Contents

The story maker . . . makes a Secondary World which your mind can enter. Inside it, what he relates is "true": it accords with the laws of that world. You therefore believe it, while you are, as it were, inside. The moment disbelief arises, the spell is broken; the magic, or rather art, has failed.

—JRR Tolkien, *On Fairy-stories*

Women oppressed by hero myths see only two choices:
Be the helpless princess sobbing for rescue, or be the knight,
helmeted and closed off in a cubicle of steel, armored against
the natural world, featureless behind a helmet.
Only men or those who act like them . . . will succeed.

—Valerie Estelle Frankel, *From Girl to Goddess*

Chapter 1

What about the Ladies?

The coffee went all over me and the floor, but thankfully not on my computer. A young woman kept apologizing profusely and saying she would buy me another coffee. She then began grabbing lots of napkins, trying to wipe me, my chair, the floor. I had to laugh.

"Hey, it's okay . . . it was an accident. No worries!"

A younger woman, who was working as a barista, came with a mop and a rag, and all was well within minutes. But apologies kept right on coming from the spiller to the now-a-bit-annoyed spillee.

She asked if she had ruined any of my work, and I said, "No, it's all good." Then she got interested and asked what I was working on. I told her I was finishing a thesis about the Heroine's Journey. She said absolutely nothing. Those long pauses can get a bit awkward, so I sat down and started collecting my papers. I was done for the day. She said she was sorry once again. Why, oh why, do women apologize so much?

She collected herself and said that she was a scriptwriter and was struggling to write about heroines. "This is just crazy that I bumped into you—literally. Sorry again." I made a mental note to not apologize for anything for the rest of the day. She continued, "I mean, I get *so* sick of gender-swapping. Filmmakers figure they can keep a masculine script and then just plop a female into it and 'look how inclusive we are.' Drives me crazy. And don't even get me started on Disney princesses!"

We sat down together, and she told me she had made a few independent short films but just couldn't get the female character right, or maybe it was the storyline that didn't fit the character. She was tired of the many female clichés and stereotypes that she found in most films. Indie films were all beginning to look alike. It's not that they were bad films, but they just didn't ring true when it came to the female. Usually, the story was told from the masculine point of view even if the female character was the lead and a strong character. "What am I doing wrong? I want to get a script out there that would be interesting for an indie producer or even Hollywood, but I also don't want to lose my integrity when it comes to female characters. I have a little girl, and I want her to see female characters that are strong or even badass, but *geez*, with those types of films, the violence is usually through the roof! Do we always have to be in combat? Or worse yet, a Disney princess just waiting for the guy to save the day. Are there any tips you can give me?"

"Uh, yeah. Let's get another cup of coffee, my friend." Needless to say, we talked for over two hours.

I understood her plight because I, too, was tired of Hollywood always using the typical masculine journey, throwing a female in the part, and calling it a day. All of my research has shown me that there is a separate and beautiful journey of the feminine: the heroine. I had written an entire thesis on the subject, and luckily, it was not ruined by flailing coffee!

The book you hold right now is the result of all the research I did about the heroine's journey as it pertains to film. After reading it, you will look at female heroic figures much differently. You'll be able to see a film and start noticing where the filmmaker got it wrong and where they got it right. When creating your scripts and films, you can add a scene here and a character there and have women loving your films, relating to your films because the female psychology works for them. Your audience will know why she did what she did. So, let me take you on a journey into the heart of the feminine—the heroine's journey.

The woman is the mother of the hero; she's the goal of the hero's achieving; she is the protectress of the hero; she is this, she is that. What more do you want?

—Joseph Campbell's response to a female student

Chapter 2

My Heroine's Journey to Find the Heroine's Journey

I uprooted four kids and moved us to southern Oregon. Was I crazy? Brave? Maybe a bit of both, but I knew I needed to be here. I'm not sure why; I just knew that I did. Sometimes I do things like that. I just know. It was that same drive and knowing that took me on my heroine's journey to find *the* heroine's journey. I just knew I needed to.

Within days of hitting Oregon, I also knew I wanted to film. I had a hunger for it; not the hunger of watching two films a night or binge-watching various series for hours on end but, being right in the messy thick of making films. I wanted to learn all I could.

I began by investing in a film called *Legends of Oz: Dorothy's Return*. The film was to be based on the book *Dorothy of*

Oz by Roger S. Baum, a great-grandson of L. Frank Baum, the creator of the original Oz series books. The story was wonderful, and I was excited. I closely followed the process of making the movie, and saw it go from a small independent film to a very large independent film with a budget of over 70 million dollars and a Hollywood cast of actors. As it grew, it strayed further and further from the book. In the end, I wasn't happy with the storyline, but maybe it would pay off. Alas, after spending $30 million on a firm to do the publicity, advertising, and distribution, the movie failed miserably on opening weekend. You can still find it on Amazon.

I learned many things from this venture, but one of the most important was that the story didn't stay true to Dorothy, the heroine. The storyline was a better fit for a hero than a heroine. Was there a difference between the two?

Still trying to learn as much as I could about film, my next adventure led me to the local community access television department. I took the necessary classes and became a studio producer. I was in heaven. There were big cameras on pedestals, lighting grids, green screens, and the most gorgeous machine of all: the mighty Tri-Caster. I couldn't get enough of it. I was determined to learn this machine, and I did. It became my baby. I directed as many shows as they would let me.

Always hungry for more, I found out that a field producer class was being offered. Oh, hell yeah, taking cameras, lights, and sound equipment out into the great outdoors to film? Sign me up. The instructor began by giving us the basics of the story. The good guys always ride in from the right of the screen, the bad guys from the left. White hats, black hats. Always film from below to elevate the subject in the eyes of the viewer. Yada, yada, yada.

Then he began to talk about Joseph Campbell's "hero's journey." Okay, got it. I knew the book, and my eldest son loved *Star Wars*. This made sense when creating a masculine story. However, he then said that the hero's journey was the human journey. *What?* I'm sorry, but I just couldn't contain myself. I blurted out, "Are you saying the hero's journey is for heroines, too?" He said, "Yup, it's for everyone. There's no difference between the heroine and the hero. They both take the same journey."

I was blindsided. I did not see that coming. It blew my little mind. I was outraged but didn't have an educated argument to continue the discussion. I had to keep my mouth shut, which was not easy for me.

What did I do? I went back to school. I was determined to find some answers about this journey of the heroine. Maybe I was wrong, and this journey of the hero *was* for everyone—but it just *couldn't* be.

Looking at all the offered classes, I felt like I was finally going to get validated by taking a scriptwriting class. Here's where they would finally agree with me and discuss the journey of the heroine—but it was a hard no. Of all the clips that we watched in that class, *not one* had a female protagonist. All of these young wannabe filmmakers were being taught about scripts through the proverbial masculine lens. I would be on my own for my research.

And research I did. I read everything I could get my

hands on that discussed the heroine. Sad to say, not much was out there that concerned film. This would be harder than I thought. No wonder we see so few films that come from the female's perspective. I changed tactics and began to look at female myths, folklore, and fairy tales, and voila, I found a gold mine. This gold mine became my thesis and now this book. I share with you all of my research: the long nights and early mornings of reading and reading and reading. Writing, rewriting, and doing it one more time.

There are guidelines for creating true heroines for the screen in the following chapters. Hopefully, you will be as excited as I was when I found out what that nasty old stepmother means for the heroine, and why all those princesses keep falling asleep. And most importantly, why every fairy godmother (and they come in all shapes and sizes) tells every heroine, "My dear, you've had the power all along..."

*[Good films] re-state transformations found in ancient
tales and make them relevant to our lives today.*

—Joan Gould, *Spinning Straw into Gold*

Chapter 3

Let's Find Your Power

In the following chapters, you are going to find where the heroine's power lies, which means you will find out where *your* power lies. You will discover new perceptions about the importance of sisters to your heroine and why the mother is usually left out of fairy tales.

The one thing this book does not give are specific definitions of masculine and feminine. Joseph Campbell uses a binary definition of these terms, and I will use the same in this book. However, I do recognize that there exists a more complex or nuanced understanding of gender. I do not suggest in any way that a female cannot take the psychological journey of the hero or that a male cannot relate to the undertaking of the heroine and her journey. The book also does not cover LGBTQ perspectives, although the numerous tales and mythologies of the LGBTQ community would provide a rich opportunity for further research. The various mythologies of the world have not left out this community. One does not have to dig very deep to find beautiful stories about lesbian, gay, bisexual, transgender, and queer individuals and their acceptance in their various cultures. The world of tales has always included LGBTQ heroes and heroines. However, this book focuses on the journey of the hero as Joseph Campbell frames it.

Before we begin this journey, some background on Joseph Campbell himself and his perception of heroines is in order. This information is in chapter 4, where you will also learn the importance of fairy tales for the heroine and the feminine psyche. These tales have been given a bad rap, and yet it was Einstein who said, "If you want to raise intelligent children, read them fairy tales."

We will begin the heroic journey itself in chapter 5. You will discover that the reason a hero takes a journey and the reason a heroine takes a journey are very different. The hero is all about the quest, while the heroine has many more reasons for her journey.

In chapter 6, we will discuss swords, daggers, and lightsabers, and the reason the heroine needs none of them. We will also look at the stereotype of women's passivity. This will be just the beginning of looking at female psychology.

The mentors whom the heroine uses will be discussed in chapter 7, and they are much different than those of the hero. The heroine typically uses only women on her journey. Her intuition is keen and usually represented by small animals. Her sisters, whether kind or mean, guide the heroine to where she needs to go. Of course, we won't leave out the importance of the wicked witch or the evil stepmother—and you will learn that they are her mentors, not monsters.

Campbell's hero goes through many trials that are metaphorical for the masculine psyche, and he assumes it is the same for the heroine. It is not. Chapter 8 tells you why she doesn't need the same types of trials. Also, she needs integration because of all those trials the darn hero goes through.

Chapter 9 goes deeper into female psychology as it relates to her heroic journey. We will discuss Freud and Jung, the Oedipus tale and complex, and my favorite archaeologist, Marija Gimbutas. A bit of science never hurt anyone!

At the end of his journey, the mighty hero returns to his community with his boon. What does the heroine come back with if she never left? In chapter 10, we will look at integration through the story of Medusa, but this perspective is through Athena's eyes, not Perseus's. We get rid of the masculine lens.

In chapter 11, we will discuss the patriarchy and how critical it is to take a look at the stories we're telling. Are they perpetuating the patriarchy? Is the male gaze in full view? Where can we, as storytellers, look to find tales that come from an equity-balanced society? This chapter has the answers for you.

Chapter 12 will give an overview of what I believe are the most critical differences between the heroine's and hero's journeys. These points can make a world of difference to your story. Women will relate, and they may not even know why. No more eye rolling when the female in the film looks at the man and says, "What do we do now?"—not for the heroine. She knows what to do, and she does not waiver because—as we now know—she's had the power all along.

Chapter 14, the bonus section, I give an analysis of four films. Here, you will find the critical portions of the heroine's journey: what the filmmakers included and what they left out.

Now let's head off on our quest to learn how to write female characters that females can relate to!

*As a female spectator we must always put ourselves
in our masculine side to be able to relate—easy enough,
it's how we live day to day.*

—Anneke Smelik, *And the Mirror Cracked*

Chapter 4

Old Joe

The dominant ways in which Hollywood studio films are written and produced are courtesy of Joseph Campbell and his mythological journey of the hero. Blockbuster films such as *Star Wars* and *Indiana Jones* have been created from his book *A Hero With a Thousand Faces*. Does this mythical journey of Campbell's include the heroine? Is there a journey that reflects her story exclusively? Can heroic stories about "real" women be created from Campbell's monomyth? Or does a female have to be at the head of an uprising or a war, such as depicted by Katniss Everdeen in *Hunger Games*, Diana Prince in *Wonder Woman*, or Jyn in *Rogue One*, to be considered a heroine? Is there a journey that reflects a heroine without her becoming a Disney princess in need of rescue by her Prince Charming? Are there guides to be used when attempting to create female-oriented scripts and films to offer audiences an authentic recognition of women characters and stories?

These questions will be answered by challenging the supposition that Joseph Campbell's mythical journey of the hero includes both men and women. Let's first take a look at Joseph Campbell himself and his thoughts on the heroine.

Joseph Campbell (1904–1987) was a professor for thirty-eight years at the all-female Sarah Lawrence College, where he taught comparative mythology. He wrote the book *A Hero with a Thousand Faces* in 1949. His premise: all cultures have hero stories that follow the same basic pattern. Campbell coined this universal pattern of the hero the "monomyth." In the book, he describes a diversity of myths, stories, fairy tales, legends, and rituals to substantiate his argument. The book did not fare well in academia, but in the late 1950s and early 1960s, artists, writers, and spiritually minded people read the book incessantly. *Hero,* as I will refer to the book from here on, became a bible of sorts for that generation, who attached to his advice of "follow your bliss," which became Campbell's renowned philosophy.

In the late 1970s, George Lucas brought Campbell's work to Hollywood by admitting that *Hero* had had a major impact on his writing of the *Star Wars* trilogy. Lucas and Campbell became friends, and at Campbell's eightieth birthday party, Lucas claimed he would still be writing the *Star Wars* trilogy if it hadn't been for Campbell's book. The success of *Star Wars* and its relation to *Hero* inspired many other directors and filmmakers to use Campbell's monomyth to create action-oriented Hollywood blockbusters. Others who have acknowledged Campbell's influence include Steven Spielberg, with the *Indiana Jones* series, and George Miller, who created *Babe* and the *Mad Max* series. Is Campbell's mythical journey strictly about the masculine hero, or does the feminine take the same journey through life with the same intentions as her male counterpart? At various times throughout *Hero*, Campbell infers that the hero can be male or female. He does use female myths and fairy tales to make various points, but they are few; when he does use them, he does not tell the complete tale, which could lead readers to conclude that the specific tale described takes on the rest of Campbell's monomyth traits, as well. There are many times in the book where the female's role in the journey is either to help the masculine hero or to become the "prize" for the hero's job well done. Campbell himself believed that women shouldn't try to be heroes, as he felt they were the symbol of the entire journey. In other words, the hero's journey was for and about the masculine hero. Nowhere in his book are there tales about menstruation or menopause, furthering the argument that his "universal" hero pattern excludes women. I believe that Campbell's mythical journey is exclusively for a male hero and that he, too, considered the journey for an adult male only. The following chapters will provide examples to substantiate this argument.

We now turn our attention to myths and fairy tales and the difference between them. In actuality, there is none. I reviewed much research by numerous scholars and concluded that there are many different definitions of myth and fairy tale, depending on the context in which each term is used. For this book, I define *myth* as how people perceive their world, and *fairy tales* as how people perceive themselves.

I want to emphasize the importance of fairy tales for the feminine journey, especially before men began rewriting them. Once men began rewriting fairy tales, the patriarchy stepped in, and the female needed to be saved. However, the old, original fairy tales began as female lore handed down from generation to generation. These tales guided women as they made natural physical and psychological transformations throughout their lives. They provided an understanding of women's psyches that were then banished by the patriarchal society. They are important, and none of the symbolism in them is trivial.

Finally, let's examine Campbell's famous monomyth, and then we will begin our journey into the feminine.

The mythological journey of Campbell's universal hero is broken into seventeen steps that reside within three larger stages. The first stage is The Departure, which includes five steps: The Call to Adventure, The Refusal of the Call, Supernatural Aid, The Crossing of the First Threshold, and The Belly of the Whale. The second stage is The Initiation, which includes six steps: The Road of Trials, The Meeting with the Goddess, Woman as Temptress, Atonement with the Father, Apotheosis, and the Ultimate Boon. The third and final stage of the journey is the Return of the Hero, which also includes six steps: Refusal of the Return, The Magic Flight, Rescue from Without, The Crossing of the Return Threshold, Master of the Two Worlds, and finally, Freedom to Live.

Not all seventeen steps need to be taken by the hero, nor do they need to be completed in a specific order. However, each stage of Campbell's universal journey is necessary for the hero to complete. The monomyth is a cycle of going and coming for the hero.

We are born to be changed . . . we are always on the move from one transformation to the next, whether we want to be transformed or not.

—*Joan Gould,* Spinning Straw into Gold

Chapter 5

Why Take a Journey in the First Place?

At times, the journey of the heroine and the hero may seem somewhat similar, but what they each seek and the reasons for the quest itself are very different. The hero's journey is all about conquest, whereas the heroine takes her journey for transformation, her family, or both. By acknowledging these differences, the writer or filmmaker can enrich the stories they choose to tell, giving the audience epic stories and mesmerizing characters from the female's point of view. Let's start at the beginning, which Campbell calls The Departure.

In the first section of Campbell's monomyth, the hero is called into his adventure. Campbell describes this call as *destiny* for the hero. A herald summons the hero to

+ one

some high historical undertaking or cultural or religious illumination. However, the example Campbell uses for this calling to adventure is the fairy tale of "The Princess and the Golden Ball."

In this tale, the young maiden goes out to play with her golden ball, which rolls away and falls into a deep, dark well. A frog tells her that he will retrieve her golden ball if she promises to take care of him and be his friend. She flippantly agrees because she wants her ball back. The frog retrieves the golden ball, and the young princess takes the ball and runs back to the castle. At dinner time, the frog enters the dining hall and tells the king that the princess agreed to take care of him. The king tells the young princess that she must keep her word. She reluctantly takes the frog up into her room, and in time the frog turns into a prince.

This fairy tale does describe the heroine's adventure; however, it is not "destiny" that calls the young princess, nor does she go out into the world to have this adventure, as Campbell's hero does. This fairy tale is symbolic of the heroine's beginning stages of transformation from young maiden to woman. Transformation is one of the triggers for the heroine to take an adventure. The frog becoming a prince symbolizes the future the young princess knows she will undertake, not destiny and the unknown, as it is for the masculine hero. Culturally, we might question whether the heroine falls in love with the frog/prince because she ultimately does not have a choice. There is a historical precedent for this: arranged marriages and young women being forced to evolve into wives and mothers before they were ready. The story is told to help guide the young woman into her future in a patriarchal society.

Cinderella stories are also heroine journeys triggered by transformation. There are over seven hundred Cinderella tales worldwide, with the oldest coming from China over one thousand years ago. These numerous tales have the maiden growing into acceptance of herself, learning that she has value, and discovering her new-found sexuality. These are not stories of a young woman being rescued by a man or about virtue being rewarded, but rather, they are stories of a maiden falling in love with herself first and then allowing the "other" into her life. This moment is portrayed when she realizes that the slipper is there, waiting to be stepped into. The maiden trapped in a tower or scrubbing floors in a castle must break free and take the journey into adulthood. Transformation is much more potent, much stronger, than the hero's call to destiny.

If transformation does not trigger the heroine's adventure, then matters related to family will do so. The recurring theme in the heroine's journey is a completed family, which heroines will risk life and health to achieve.

As discussed in chapter 4, fairy tales began as female oral storytelling handed down generation to generation before they were ever in written form, so there are many more sisters saving brothers and daughters rescuing fathers than the reverse. In the Danish tale of *The Wild Swans*, Eliza weaves coats of stinging nettle and gives up her voice to save her brothers from the spell put on them by their evil stepmother. In the tale of *Beauty and the Beast*, Belle feels the need to save her father from the beast. In the film *The Hunger Games*, Katniss Everdeen protects her younger sister by volunteering herself to partake in the deadly games, thus beginning her adventure. A female will not take an adventure unless her family is at stake or she is in a transformative part of her life. There is no call of destiny for the heroine, as Campbell claims there is for the hero.

Campbell writes that the hero may refuse the call at first or, at times, dismiss it all together. If he dismisses it, the adventure is not taken, and he may feel he has missed something throughout his life. An example of this refusal is Luke Skywalker telling Obi-Wan Kenobi that he, Luke, cannot become a Jedi. He must stay at home and help his aunt and uncle. Destiny is calling young Skywalker and he wants to go, but he refuses the call. However, destiny prevails, and he goes on to become a Jedi and take his many adventures of conquest. Compare this to Katniss Everdeen in *The Hunger Games*, who wants to take care of her mother and younger sister even though her friend Gale begs her to leave. Yet, when her younger sister is chosen as a "tribute," Katniss volunteers herself, and she begins her journey. Luke Skywalker is called by destiny and his desire for conquest; Katniss is called by family—saving her younger sister. The distinction between the two is important to remember when you are creating your heroine's journey.

When writing stories, scripts, or creating films, remember that the hero's journey is about destiny and conquest, whereas the heroine's journey is triggered by her own physical and psychological transformations or saving family in some way. Family is of the utmost importance to the heroine, although our patriarchal society has devalued this trait. Regarding transformation from young maiden to woman, one may think of the numerous Disney princess movies. Many are based on old fairy tales and feminine lore. However, no one man has destroyed the beautiful female teaching tales more than Walt Disney. In America, when adolescent girls think of fairy tales, sadly, they think of the versions created by Disney. When these stories are looked at with a patriarchal bias, as Disney did, the female symbolism gets lost. At times, the entire psychological perspective of the tale gets changed. The heroine's journey of transformation and growth morphs into the hero's story of conflict or conquest. These films are the ones most women reject because they objectify and minimize women.

Stories concerning the heroine's transformation make psychological sense to the feminine psyche: transitioning from maiden to woman, from woman to motherhood, and finally to the older wise woman. Women understand and can relate to these transformations, and they will always spark an adventure for your heroine. Also, remember how extremely important family is to the heroine. Many stories have been created around the heroine doing what is needed to save a family member. Give your heroine a reason, one that the feminine psyche can relate to, to do what she does.

In the next chapter we will take a look at all those weapons that the true heroine does not need, as well as the sleeping princess that seems to be waiting for a kiss.

A woman has a profound capacity to be still, perhaps the most powerful act any human being can make. She is required to go back to a very still inner center every time something profound happens to her. This is a highly creative act.... She is... receptive, not passive.

—Robert Johnson, SHE: Understanding Female Psychology

Chapter 6

We Are *Not* Passive

In chapter 5 we saw that the heroine cannot simply say no to transformation the way a hero can say no to destiny and his journey. However, she may be able to put it on hold. The old tales allow the maiden, mother, or crone the time necessary to make the transformations needed. The true heroine neither uses nor needs a dagger or sword to achieve her goals as does Campbell's masculine hero. Her weapons are those only the feminine understands. Although she seldom uses violence, our heroine is definitely *not* sitting around waiting to be saved by anyone.

Let's start by looking at all of those sleeping heroines. The metaphorical deep sleep, or chrysalis state, is a symbol for the temporary dismissal of the heroine's transformative journey. We can recognize this symbol in tales such as *Sleeping Beauty*, *Snow White*, and Dorothy in *The Wizard of Oz.* Campbell mentions sleep in *Hero*; however, his interpretation is not from a female perspective. He writes that the heroine is protected in her virginity and caught up in her adolescence. She does not need protection, nor is she caught up in anything. This is transformation, and it is the first of many transformational journeys our heroine will take.

In the tale of *Little Briar Rose*, Campbell writes that Briar Rose sleeps for many years, until a prince comes to wake her. However, in the tale *The Sleeping Beauty in the Wood* by Charles Perrault, written long before *Little Briar Rose*, the young heroine awakens on her own after the 100-year spell is over. She looks up at the prince standing over her and tells him that he must have been waiting a long, long time for her. She wasn't waiting to be rescued by a prince; *he* was waiting for *her*.

In the tale of *Snow White*, the heroine's chrysalis state is caused by the poisoned red apple. The symbolism brimming in this tale is emphasized in Joan Gould's book *Spinning Straw into Gold* which I highly recommend. For example, the colors red, white, black, and gold are significant in the story; they are the colors of transformation. White symbolizes innocence, and red represents the loss of that innocence. Black is the knowledge that must be gained through the transformation, and gold represents the final step in that transformation. Gould's analysis of the tale is that the poison inside the apple is feminine knowledge concerning virginity and fertility and the ultimate loss of both; childbirth and motherhood and the extreme pain of both; and the cycle of life and death. It is no wonder that Snow White collapses! However, in the original tale, Snow

White does not swallow the apple; it becomes lodged in her throat. When a wandering prince sees her lying in her glass coffin, he has his servants pick up the coffin, which dislodges the apple. Snow White wakes on her own accord and wonders where she is. She is wondering where she is in her life at this time of transformation. According to Gould, the prince is a metaphor for the possibilities that lie ahead of her. No heroine needs love's first kiss to awaken from her own transformation.

The metaphorical sleep allows the heroine the time *she* needs to go through the transformative time of adolescence. It allows her the time needed for her emotions to catch up with her body. When she has gone through her transformation, she wakes ready to take the necessary steps toward womanhood. *She* knows when the time is right for her. Mind you, she isn't saying no to her journey, just postponing it until *she* is ready. The heroine holds the power over her own transformative times in life. This is true for older women as well. Sleep is the symbol of rebirth, and the heroine will hide or sleep to aid in her transformation. There is not a man anywhere who can stop it or initiate it. Remember that the sleeping heroine's story is her own, not the hero's.

Another distinction between the journeys of the heroine and the hero is the use of weaponry and violence. Campbell's hero has been bestowed with supernatural powers and weapons to accomplish his feat. Young Prince Five Weapons is clad with his powerful fists, a bow and arrows, a sword, a club, and a thunderbolt. King Arthur, clad in armor, has the mighty sword Excalibur, while Luke Skywalker of Star Wars was given his father's lightsaber.

Instead of being clad in armor and carrying a sword, the heroine is clad with her own feminine powers and feminine talismans. The body of feminine symbolism and meanings is large, and there are numerous books pertaining to just this subject. The following are a few examples, but the main point is that the heroine has no need for weapons, as the hero does. If you are involved in a film or see a film that has the heroine slashing a sword or having one-on-one combat, she is in the midst of a masculine journey and has lost her power of the feminine.

The heroine can be found with magic keys, rings, mirrors, combs, magic hoops, or the ability to weave and spin as she heads into her adventure. According to Valerie Estelle Frankel, who wrote the fascinating book entitled *From Girl to Goddess*, anything round is from the feminine realm. It represents the female's fertile life cycle, and therein lies her power. The moon, Mother Earth, an egg, a spiral, and of course the womb are all examples of feminine symbolism. Wonder woman had her round lasso, not a straight spear. Objects from the home and kitchen are symbolically feminine. Dorothy accidently melts the Wicked Witch of the West using water from a bucket and mop. Rumpelstiltskin rides away on a soup ladle. Weaving is also a feminine symbol and holds power for the heroine. Grandmother Spider weaves together all of the interconnections in the many indigenous stories about her. The tale of Philomela has her weaving information to her sister after she is raped, and her tongue cut out so together they could get revenge. Young Eliza stitches stinging nettles together to save her brothers. The symbolism in female fairy tales and myths is overwhelming. Absolutely nothing is trivial. When creating films about heroines, learn as much as you can about female symbolism, and use it. The women who watch may not pick up on it consciously, but their subconscious definitely will.

If a heroine does need to use a weapon, it is usually a long-distance type. Katniss Everdeen in *The Hunger Games* and Susan in *The Chronicles of Narnia* have bows; the original Wonder Woman has a lasso. In the Pueblo tradition, Yellow Woman has many adventures; she uses her courage to act in times of great peril, and her triumph is achieved by her sensuality, not through violence and destruction. The lack of weaponry and violence is a major difference between the hero and heroine journeys. It just doesn't feel right for the heroine to be in one-on-one combat, and no old tales depict this for her. She uses other means to win her metaphorical battles, whether they be with wicked witches or the goddess Aphrodite. When you see a heroine wielding a sword or lightsaber, she is taking a hero's journey and is very much in her masculine side.

Heroines are not passive, although it may seem that way at times. What looks like sleep or hiding out in a tower is actually transformation and integration. These take courage and fortitude, and the heroine has both. She does not usually accomplish her journey with weapons or violence, but that does not mean she just idly sits. The many old myths and tales never confuse the woman's domain with passivity. When you are creating stories and films, remember the wit, intuitive skills, symbolism, valor, and ingenuity of your heroine, and use them.

The next chapter discusses the many mentors the heroine needs to accomplish her goals. Some may surprise you.

I am who she is not. She is both what I would most aspire to be but feel I never can be and what I am most proud not to be but fearful of becoming.

—Christine Downing, *Psyche's Sisters,*
Re-Imagining the Meaning of Sisterhood

Chapter 7

"I Got Your Back, Girl" – the Heroine's Mentors

In this chapter we will discuss the support that the heroine needs in order to accomplish her transition or to protect and save her family. We all need support, and the heroine is no different. However, she differs from the hero in who she chooses and needs to give her the support on her heroic journey.

According to Campbell, the hero who has accepted his adventure must meet someone to give him support and help him throughout his journey. Many female examples are given because, in Campbell's journey of the hero, women protect the hero's destiny. They are the guiding force for his journey. Examples given are Spider-Woman, Mother Nature, the Cosmic Mother, and the thread of Ariadne.

These females are all present to support the male hero on his journey, yet all of these protectors have their own journey and story to tell. The hero also has male mentors with supernatural powers and weapons that are bestowed upon him. These mentors stay with him for all or only part of the journey. King Arthur has Merlin as his magician, and Luke Skywalker has Obi-Wan Kenobi and then Yoda as his Jedi trainers.

In stories about heroines, they are given support from other females, because the masculine has no advice to give concerning the feminine journeys of transformation or saving the family. Examples of the benevolent feminine supporting the heroine include the Hopi story of a young Payupki girl. Spider Grandmother gives her magic medicine to put on her legs so she can win the race against the boy from the bad-hearted male Tikuvi clan. When the young boy runner transforms into a dove, Spider Grandmother tells a hawk to knock the dove down. The young heroine wins the race and brings honor to her family and female tribe. The story of Cinderella features a fairy godmother who creates needed ball gowns and glass slippers. The Chinese version of this tale, *Cam and Tam*, has the Goddess of Mercy, who gives the girl a fish to befriend and care for. In the Russian tale *Vasilisa*, the young maiden has a doll that can speak and give wise advice, which her dying mother had given to her. All of these stories symbolize the hope given to a young maiden by another female when the psyche is overwhelmed with transformation. There are female mentors for the older heroine as well. In the film *A Price Above Rubies*, a young mother is always bumping into an old beggar woman who shares stories and asks questions that the heroine needs to hear in order to live the life she is meant to live.

Not all aid given to the heroine is supportive and full of kindly wisdom. The heroine also comes up against female mentors who are not so kind but who are still brimming with knowledge the young heroine will need in her journey. The wicked witch and evil stepmother are there to teach the young maiden independence. That's right, these darker characters are there to give the heroine the push she needs to grow up and get out in the world. Who would ever leave Oz if she had the opportunity to stay with Glinda the Good Witch of the South? Metaphorically, the darker characters are there to push the heroine into adulthood when she may not want to go. The psyche needs to evolve, and these female evil witches and stepmothers give the heroine the push she needs. The young heroine hasn't been out in the world yet. To her, the world is a dark, mysterious forest, yet she can only grow and transform by an encounter with that world, so sometimes, something or someone has to push her out into it.

The Wicked Witch of the West pushes Dorothy to decide what she wants. *How important is it to you? Let me tell you what it takes to be queen of a castle. It's time to sink or swim, my pretty!* In the film, Snow White's evil stepmother pushes her out into the dark forest, but in the written tale she goes to Snow White three different times to teach the lessons needed. The first time, the evil stepmother comes as the old beggar lady, she is selling pretty stay-laces. The second time, she comes selling beautiful combs. These encounters represent Snow White's longing to become a woman, yet she is left unconscious after each encounter, representing that her psyche is not quite ready. Once again, there is nothing trivial in fairy tales. Symbolism and female psychology abound in all of these tales.

Another important mentor the heroine has that Campbell's hero does not are the heroine's sisters. Campbell does not mention brothers at all in *Hero,* possibly because they are not part of nor important to the hero's journey. The only female tales where sisterhood is not abundantly found are the Greek goddess myths. Goddesses are immortal, making them immune to the normal stages of life. They do not need the sister-sister bond to help navigate the intricacies of the numerous transformations that mortal women go through.

Fairy tales, however, are overflowing with the heroine's need for sister mentorship. These tales connect her to age-old wisdom, reminders of a matrifocal culture. They may preserve reminders of a mythological tradition older than the officially preserved one. Sisters give women power and represent women as a group, which is much more powerful than the individual heroine. The heroine needs the strength represented by her sisters to face the patriarchy. There are too many stories and tales that include the heroine's sisters to think they are irrelevant.

The heroine is usually the youngest and most beautiful of three sisters. In tales, such as Eros and Psyche and the numerous versions of Beauty and the Beast stories, her jealous sisters push her to try and find out who she has wed. In the Cinderella stories, she has stepsisters who taunt her with their plans to go to the ball, creating in her a desire to also go. Bluebeard tales depict the older sisters warning the heroine not to marry. From a psychological perspective, sisters are there to awaken the consciousness in the heroine. They have the knowing that the young maiden lacks, which is why she is usually portrayed as the youngest. Just as with the wicked witch or stepmother, the sisters are at times represented as dark or mean characters, pushing the heroine to do what is needed. In other tales, they warn the heroine of evil that lurks just up ahead of her. Metaphorically, they represent her intuition or subconscious.

The final set of mentors the heroine has are the little animals and birds that are there just when she needs them. Some consider these creatures as being a part of the heroine. They are there to comfort and help when the task is too hard, or the psyche is overwhelmed. They are her intuitive voice telling her where to go or what to stay away from. Disney has trivialized these important figures in the heroine's journey. In the film *Moana*, creatures are used strictly for jokes. But in the old tales, they have an important role to play for the heroine. Psyche could not have gotten through her many tasks without the help of ants, reeds, and other helpers. When the filmmaker understands the symbolism of these many characters, the story will change and become much more interesting and enriching.

One must remember that this journey of the heroine is a psychological one and that most of the characters are metaphorical, but it pays to know what each represents for the feminine psyche. All heroines need hope, and it is usually represented in the form of a fairy godmother of some sort. The evil stepmother or wicked witch can give the heroine the push she needs to grow up or the knowledge of what it will take to become queen of her own castle. She needs these invaluable lessons. The many creatures that are there for the heroine also guide her and support her.

Finally, the importance of sisters to a heroine's journey cannot be overemphasized. Disney has all but gotten rid of these mentors. How will the young heroine know the ropes without them? They can be mean stepsisters or kind older sisters, but they represent the heroine's need to know about the feminine ways that her fairy godmother is just too uncomfortable to tell her. Use sisters in your stories. They can come in the form of best friends, aunties, female cousins, or actual sisters. Every heroine needs her many female mentors.

In the next chapter, we will discuss feminine initiations and heroic trials. We will examine both by using the very old tale of Eros and Psyche, which is an inset story from *The Metamorphoses of Apuleius*.

Traditional psychology is often spare or entirely silent about deeper issues important to women: the archetypal, the intuitive, the sexual and cyclical, the ages of women, a woman's way, a woman's knowing, her creative fire.

—Clarissa Pinkola Estés, *Women Who Run with the Wolves*

Chapter 8

Initiations and Integration – Let's Get Real about the Patriarchy

In this chapter we will dive into the phase of Campbell's monomyth called The Initiation as it relates to the heroine's journey. The entire initiation phase includes The Road of Trials, Meeting with the Goddess, Woman as Temptress, Atonement with the Father, Apotheosis, and Ultimate Boon. Some of these steps will be explained in chapters 9 and 10. This chapter discusses the marriage initiation and the trials.

Although, The Road of Trials comes before Meeting with the Goddess in Campbell's monomyth, here we will describe the feminine initiation for the heroine first. Both of these sections will be described using the tale of Eros and Psyche, but the heroine's initiation comes before her trials in the tale. We will start at the beginning for Psyche and then provide context for the trials that she must endure to save the family she has decided she wants.

Campbell argues that the masculine journey to marry the mythical goddess is the same for a maiden. Examples given are the story of the Frog Prince when the frog turns into a prince, Psyche being bestowed with immortality, and the Virgin Mary being taken to the bridal chamber in Heaven. All of these examples have the powerless heroine waiting for the man to rescue her from the bleak life she has. This response is typical when female tales are analyzed through male bias. A passive heroine meets male fantasies about femininity. As we have seen in previous chapters, the heroine is not powerless; this is her life, and she will take charge of it. In the original tale of the princess and the frog, the frog did not turn into a prince until the princess threw it against the wall, demonstrating her individual power. Psyche was not bestowed with immortality but, rather, earns her admittance into the world of gods and goddesses.

For the heroine, the marriage initiation is much different from Campbell's description of the masculine hero marrying the "goddess" and winning his ultimate prize. The most common tales that describe the marriage initiation for women are the folktales of type 425 C, *Beauty and the Beast*. The young maiden finds herself with a beast or animal of some sort who wants her for his wife. There are also many Bluebeard tales in which the maiden realizes that once she has married her prince, he becomes a monster, and she needs to escape from him or lose her life.

The most commonly known of these stories, *Beauty and the Beast*, written by French author Jeanne-Marie Leprince de Beaumont, is based on the story of Eros and Psyche. The latter tale was written by second-century Latin poet Apuleius as an inset story of a larger tale called *Metamorphoses* or *The Golden Ass*. Although Campbell uses portions of the Eros and Psyche tale in *Hero* as an example of the Road of Trials, he does not tell the beginning of the tale. The feminine marriage initiation will be described using this tale because it is one of the oldest tales with this motif, and many other tales come from it. The synopsis below is based on Robert A. Johnson's book *SHE: Understanding Female Psychology*.

In the tale of Eros and Psyche, a king has three daughters. The father is the key player in most of these tales because, symbolically, the heroine is giving up one man for another. Psyche is the youngest and fairest of the three daughters. The oldest two daughters marry, but intimidated by her beauty, men will not come near Psyche. The father consults the Oracle, who says that Psyche will marry something so terrible as to be death itself. Psyche is to be taken to a mountaintop and chained to a rock, where she will await her beast. The procession that takes Psyche to the mountaintop is filled with tears and sadness.

This act is rich in female symbolism, with Eurocentric wedding customs coming from this part of the tale. Marriage is the metaphor for the death of the maiden's life with her family of birth, and for the maiden, the procession to the altar is similar to the death procession. The groom awaits to abduct her and take her to a new life to create a new family. Tears flow as the maiden bride buries her old life for the new one that lies ahead of her. Here, marriage is both death and resurrection for a woman. This is not the case for Campbell's hero. For him, the bride is a possession or prize.

Psyche is left, chained and alone in the dark of night, awaiting her beast. Aphrodite, the goddess of love, beauty, pleasure, and procreation, is jealous and annoyed at the beauty and perfection of Psyche, much like the wicked queen in *Snow White*. She sends her young son, Eros, god of love, to shoot his arrow of love into Psyche to make sure she will fall in love with the beast, who is to find her. Once Eros sees Psyche, he, too, is captivated by her beauty, and accidentally pricking himself on his own arrow, he falls in love with her. He brings her to his beautiful castle, where she awakens in what she feels is paradise. Eros only visits her at night, when it is dark, and she is forbidden to look at him. During the day, she has the rule of the castle, where all her needs are met. This scenario is also played out in *Beauty and the Beast, East of the Sun West of the Moon, The Green Serpent*, and many others.

Psyche is happy in her new relationship but misses her family. She pleads with Eros to let her sisters come to the castle. He says they will cause trouble for their relationship. She continues to plead and finally wins Eros over, and the sisters are allowed to visit her. They tell her that for all she knows, her husband may be a monster, and she had better find out who this monster is before it is too late. They devise a plan to have Psyche light a lamp and look at Eros as he sleeps, even though Psyche has been told not to look upon him. She does as she is told by her sisters and sees that she is married not to a monster but to the god of love himself.

She realizes her blunder, but just at that moment, a drop of wax falls on Eros, waking him. He tells Psyche that they can no longer be together and that the child she bears will be a girl instead of a god, then he takes flight back to his mother, Aphrodite. Psyche's paradise has been destroyed by listening to her sisters.

As discussed in the previous chapter, the importance of the heroine's sisters is often overlooked by male analysts. Men are terrified of the aspect of feminine energy that sisters represent. Psyche's sisters encourage her to question paradise, whereas Eros wants to keep her in the dark. If she just does as she is told, Eros will stay, her child will be born an immortal god, and she will continue to live in paradise. However, Psyche (the Greek word for "soul") needs to grow and transform from a naïve maiden to a wise, nurturing mother. The symbolism of the lamp is Psyche seeing her husband for who he really is and removing the deception. This also applies to Eros seeing that Psyche is no longer the naïve maiden whom he hoped she would continue to be.

After Eros leaves Psyche, she is devastated. She has decided that Eros is her family, and, as we discussed in chapter 5, the heroine will do whatever is needed to reunite her family. She goes to every god to seek help in finding Eros, yet none will help. Her last hope is Aphrodite herself. After giving Psyche a good talking-to, she sets in motion the tasks that Psyche must accomplish if she is to ever be with Eros again. Symbolically, these tasks have nothing to do with Eros and everything to do with Psyche's transformation into a wise woman and mother. Aphrodite is the wicked mother-in-law giving Psyche the push she needs to grow up.

The tasks Aphrodite demands of Psyche make profound psychological statements. They are usually what the male focuses on when analyzing these types of tales, and of course, Campbell does focus on them. But as we have learned, Psyche's growth does not begin with the trials she undertakes; that honor goes to her sisters, who are vital to her first push toward transforming from maiden to wife to mother. Jungian analyst and author Robert A. Johnson's version of Psyche's tasks and his view of their symbolic meaning, from his book *She: Understanding Female Psychology*, are used for the following synopsis.

Aphrodite demands the sorting of seeds for Psyche's first task, knowing she cannot possibly do this. Ants come to her rescue, which symbolically represents her sisters coming to her aid. Johnson suggests that this task also symbolizes a woman's need to differentiate in life, both in the home and in her professional life. Organizational skills are imperative for keeping order and not collapsing into chaos. Johnson says they are of quiet quality, instinctual, not of the intellect, and only available to women.

The second task is the collecting of fleece. This time, reeds give Psyche their sage advice. They tell her to wait until evening and collect only the small amount of fleece she will need to satisfy Aphrodite's demands. The tell her to not collect it from the aggressive rams themselves but from the branches and fencing that snagged the rams earlier in the day. This act symbolizes that aggressive masculine power is not always useful and can cause trouble. Use the power needed but keep it in proportion to what is necessary at any specific time.

For the third task, Psyche is asked to fill a crystal goblet with water from the heavily guarded River Styx, which falls from the tallest mountaintop and drops down into the underworld before cycling up again. An eagle sent by Zeus helps Psyche by taking the vessel, flying into an unguarded area of the river, and getting the water for her. This is a metaphor for the female to always look at the big picture of life, take the knowledge, and have an eagle eye for what needs to be accomplished.

The fourth and final task required of Psyche is to go into the underworld, secure Persephone's Box of Beauty, and bring it back to Aphrodite. Feeling defeated before she even starts, Psyche climbs a tower and is ready to throw herself off when the tower speaks to her. While Psyche alone must face Persephone, the tower gives her advice on and directions for entering and exiting the underground. After achieving her goal, Psyche returns to the human world, where she opens the forbidden box—just as she had used the forbidden lamp and gazed upon Eros. She immediately collapses into a metaphorical deep sleep. This triggers Eros, who flies to her, pricks her with his arrow of love, and awakens her. Psyche completes her journey by giving the box to Aphrodite, while Eros convinces Zeus that he and Psyche must marry. Zeus agrees to this; he also makes Psyche immortal. Their child is born a female, and they name her Pleasure.

There are many different interpretations of what this fourth and final task symbolizes for the heroine. The usual male interpretation is women's obsession with beauty, vanity, and the danger of narcissism. Johnson's analysis is that the box held the feminine "secret mystery . . . the essence of that feminine quality that must remain a mystery, certainly to men." Psyche took it for herself and became "unconscious," unable to complete her spiritual journey. Only true love—the prick from Eros's arrow— could awaken her and allow her to complete her journey.

Marie-Louise von Franz, a student of Jung and author of numerous books on female fairy tales and their symbolism, interprets the fourth task much differently. Beginning with the symbolism of the ointment inside the Box of Beauty itself, she writes that in Egyptian times, creamy ointments were used to anoint statues of the gods. The ointments were metaphors for life, or a psychic substance that the gods needed. In Christianity, von Franz writes, holy oil is used to anoint the Holy Ghost unto followers so they may receive the "ultimate spiritual devotion." It makes sense that the ointment would belong to an immortal goddess and not a human girl. Christine Downing's perspective in *Psyche's Sisters: Reimagining the Meaning of Sisterhood* is that the box symbolizes "the beauty to which Persephone but not Aphrodite has access . . . the beauty that comes with an intimate inner knowledge of death—the ultimate beauty of the psyche."

Both Downing and von Franz do not think the ending of Eros and Psyche rings true. Downing writes that immortality for Psyche brings her back to where she was at the beginning of the story, "exalted above all women." Von Franz writes that the ending was created for the story to fit in with the rest of the tales included in *The Golden Ass of Apuleius*.

I like the tale of Eros and Psyche because it demonstrates not only the transformation of Psyche from maiden to woman and mother, but it also shows how the heroine will do whatever is needed for her family.

Another story in *Hero* as an example for the Road of Trials is the Sumerian myth of the goddess Inanna, who ruled the Earth and the heavens. This story is included here because it describes the trials that Inanna must take and the integration that the heroine must make. We will explore these more closely in chapters 9 and 10.

Inanna descends into the world of no return to meet her sister, Ershkigal, the goddess of the Underworld. At each of the seven gates that Inanna must descend through, she is to remove a portion of her clothing. Clothes represent what is going on internally for the heroine. In this case, Inanna must be stripped of her jewelry, her breastplate, and her gown before she is allowed to enter the underworld. Metaphorically, she is psychologically naked; she is no longer a great goddess but a sister.

Campbell's interpretation of the myth has Inanna, as the light, facing her sister, who is the dark. He writes that regardless of male or female, darkness represents the shadow side of the individual. This is the point in the hero's adventure at which the hero's masculine ego must be put to death. However, there is no shadow side of the female that must be put to death. This story is about Inanna's integration of the part of every woman that has been suppressed or banished to the underground in order to live in a patriarchal society. As Valerie Estelle Frankel describes in *From Girl to Goddess: The Heroine's Journey through Myth and Legend,* "the dark sister, buried in so many women, must be faced and confronted in the underworld to which she's been banished."

The Road of Trials is where the action lies for the masculine hero. Campbell writes that this step has produced literature of epic proportions. The hero is going out into the world slaying dragons, while the heroine's action is usually nonviolent but can be just as powerful for her journey. Her tests include perseverance, patience, inner strength, and trust. We find our heroine sorting seeds, gathering wool, stitching a tapestry, sewing coats of stinging nettles, and finding water to support her village.

There is never a time when Psyche is asked to slay a dragon, fight an ogre, or shoot stormtroopers to achieve what she wants. The female has nothing to learn from those skills. The tasks of the heroine teach her to grow and be powerful when needed, usually in a nonviolent way. Although the many tasks the heroine accomplishes seem tedious and passive, as with the metaphorical deep sleep, they give the heroine a chance to either integrate her experiences or continue with her female transformations in life. They may not be action-oriented, but they are powerful.

The marriage initiation sees the heroine transforming from maiden to woman. The tale of Eros and Psyche has given forth many tales of transformation for the heroine. This tale also emphasizes the importance of the heroine's mentors, especially her sisters.

In the next chapter we will look more closely into feminine psychology. We will see where Jung and Freud got it wrong about the feminine psyche, leading to a patriarchal bias in many tales. We will also dig deeper to see why the heroine does not need the hierarchal climb to godhood. She was born a goddess; she just needs to remember.

*We may find ourselves wondering to what degree
the suppression of women's rites has actually been
the suppression of women's rights.*

—Merlin Stone, *When God was a Woman*

Chapter 9

The Heroine and Female Psychology – Freud and Jung Have Issues

In this chapter, we will take a deep dive into female psychology as it pertains to Campbell's Atonement step in his monomyth. Then we will look to understand Campbell's Apotheosis step as it pertains to the heroine.

The Atonement Stage is the symbolic conquering of the father or authority figure. According to Campbell, the father is the one who intrudes into the child's paradise and the original protection of the mother. The father becomes the competition and the archetypal enemy. For the hero, the ego is the metaphorical father that must be released. However, for the heroine, the mother cannot be the competition or her enemy. The male and female heroic journeys take a different path once again.

According to Campbell, the son must master or conquer his father; however, he also writes that the daughter must master or conquer the mother. He makes this analysis from the perspective of male psychology. According to Elina M. Reenkola, a Finnish psychoanalysis, scholar, and author of the book *The Veiled Female Core*, the daughter's journey is not to master or conquer the mother, because the mother has "all the good the girl wishes for herself, . . . [and] the longing for an omnipotent mother remains with us even throughout adulthood." The heroine cannot master or conquer the mother because her own psyche will not allow it; one does not "conquer" good. According to Reenkola, there are no tales that represent this for the female. The daughter needs to separate and individuate from the mother, yet it is extremely difficult because of the female's complete identification with her. Reenkola goes on to write that Freud's research on this subject gives attention only to patricide, or the boy's separation from his father, and then assumes it is the same for the female. The act of matricide is extremely rare in fairy tales and myths, as it is in reality. According to Reenkola, there is not a single tale or myth where the heroine herself kills her mother, even when the mother is being represented in the form of the mean stepmother or wicked witch.

This now brings us to Freud's Oedipal complex. The myth of Oedipus tells the story of a boy who unknowingly kills his father and then marries his mother. Campbell is correct when he shows that this myth is quite universal for the masculine hero; however, it does not apply to the heroine. A myth or fairy tale in which the female murders her mother and marries her father does not exist. Both boys and girls have their Oedipal rivals, but according to Reenkola, the boy's rival—the father—has not been his caretaker. The girl's rival, her mother, is also her caretaker, the one who feeds her and has given her life. As noted earlier, the mother possesses all the good the girl wants for herself. This setting forms the predicament that the female finds herself in as she grows into adulthood. The numerous fears and guilt the girl has to work through concerning her mother are beyond the scope of this book and not particularly relevant here. The important point is Campbell does not recognize that attaining womanhood is much more complex for a girl than growing to manhood is for the boy. The lack of female myths and Campbell's incorrect interpretations of female psychology emphasize that the heroine has a very different journey from the hero.

The Apotheosis stage in Campbell's monomyth is about the hero's hierarchal climb to godhood. The heroine's quest is much different. She does not take a journey to ultimately attain a patriarchal divine state but to reintegrate the parts of herself that the patriarchal way of life has shattered or suppressed. The heroine's personal journey is inward, to find and regain her lost personal power over life and death.

The heroine is trying to reintegrate the sense of the true feminine state, but the patriarchal society does not recognize or approve of this state. However, there was a time historically when this feminine state was a normal part of society. To fully understand the heroine's journey concerning the metaphorical goddess way of life, the work of archeologist and anthropologist Marija Gimbutas must be introduced.

Marija Gimbutas was an archaeologist and cultural anthropologist. She was born in Lithuania but did much of her research and teaching in America. In her book, *The Civilization of the Goddess,* Gimbutas examines the life, social structures, and religion of Old Europe dating from 3,000 to 7,000 years ago. She describes these various civilizations and state that the art found from this era was devoid of any type of weaponry symbolism. There were no scenes depicting conflict or fighting, or of war or torture. The people in Old Europe transitioned from being small clans of food gatherers to agricultural communities to finally, in 4,000 to 3,500 BC, there were towns of ten thousand people with smaller communities surrounding the larger towns. There were no archaeological signs of any fortresses or protective walls of any type. These communities were not located or built for defense

Gimbutas also showed that religion played an important role in these societies, in which social structure and worship were intertwined. The female-oriented Old Europe societies were organized around a theocratic communal temple, with a governing council of women. Burial evidence does not show any imbalance between the sexes. Gimbutas claims that the deity for Paleolithic as well as Neolithic life was female, creating a matrilineal and matrifocal society, not a matriarchal society, as once was assumed. There has not been any archaeological evidence of a father god.

An important point about Gimbutas's findings is that previous scholars did not think religion of that specific time was relevant, and when investigating the artifacts, they looked through the biased eyes of patriarchy. Many sites had to be reevaluated because of this bias.

The demise of this peaceful way of life began with the invasion of nomadic bands seeking grass for their herds. These people were male-dominant, with male gods, and had a hierarchic social structure. Gradually, the landscape changed, and fortifications were built where there were once peaceful settlements. Material wealth was acquired through technologies of destruction rather than technologies of production. The foundation for Western civilization was being laid. The beginning of slavery came from this period and these people. Graves began to change; the people started including bows, arrows, knives, and spears in them. Physical devastation and cultural impoverishment came with each wave of invasions. The powerful and violent invaders imposed their patriarchal culture and religion on these people. Slowly, the attributes of the one great goddess was broken into pieces and transitioned into lesser and separate goddesses. Each goddess received a unique attribute that had once belonged to the one goddess completely. The people were ruled under one god, and his name was Zeus. For the first time, rape became a norm in mythology. The last society to hold on to the peaceful matrifocal way of life lived on the island of Crete, which finally fell 3,200 years ago.

According to Jean Shinoda Bolen, author of *Goddesses in Every Woman,* Greek goddesses are fragments of a one-time, all-encompassing goddess. Once the patriarchal way of life was solidified in society, the masculine feared the wisdom of the crone and banished her to the metaphorical underworld. The maiden and mother archetypes were easily oppressed without the wisdom of the crone. This has created the psychological split for women, with society vilifying the most powerful part of the female's divinity. Part of the heroine's journey is to reintegrate this feminine wisdom and make herself psychologically whole once again.

These descriptions should give you a small grasp of female psychology. The most important point is that the feminine psyche is different from the masculine psyche. The symbolism of the mother and her impact on the heroine is of utmost importance. This is why you do not see many mothers in fairy tales. A mother figure yes, but the actual mother, no. They are the good in the world, what every heroine will herself eventually become after much integration and transformation.

Archaeology shows us that the heroine has no need to climb a hierarchal ladder to godhood. The goddess nature is something that every woman holds within her, and every woman needs to begin to claim this. Storytellers show the darkness that women suppress and how it can come into the light. There are many myths that tell this story. In chapter 8, the story of the goddess Inanna showed how women can claim the portions of themselves that have been suppressed by the patriarchal society. When a woman who is tired of being told that she is not good enough for a job in a predominantly masculine field stands up and screams

"*No more*," her suppressed goddess is coming to light. We need to have these stories told.

In the next chapter, we will examine the story of Medusa and Athena and how they use the raging fury of the patriarchy to achieve their integration and freedom.

We are not only subjected to power; we also have the potential and the power to become a subject different from the one we were socially programmed to become if only we want to, and if the social circumstances are favorable.

—Anneke Smelik, *And the Mirror Cracked*

Chapter 10

What's Our Boon? What Can We Bring Back When We Never Left? Ask Medusa

This chapter covers Campbell's Ultimate Boon and the last stage of the hero's journey, The Return. The main focus of this chapter relates to why the heroine takes a journey in the first place. She may never have to leave or come back to accomplish her goals.

The Ultimate Boon step of Campbell's journey describes what the hero gains on his journey into the unknown and what he brings back to his community. The heroine does not bring anything back to the community; in most tales, the heroine does not have to leave to complete her journey. "Boon" is not the appropriate word for the accomplishment of the heroine's journey. For the heroine, the reuniting of family, transformation, or the full integration of self is what she ultimately accomplishes. The purpose of the male hero's quest is to conquer; the heroine quests to create a family. One may argue that this is demeaning for the heroine, but the patriarchy has devalued motherhood and what it takes, physically and psychologically, to transform from maiden to mother. The societal assumption is that woman's ability to nurture is a natural drive, that there is no need for reciprocity. The woman is placed in a self-sacrificing position because of this, and she then does not realize how much of herself she is giving up by denying the needs she may have.

The hero returns from whence he came a different person or with some exalted knowledge to share among those left behind. The return also includes the need to integrate the two worlds. The hero is battling his own ego and is the champion of things becoming. Campbell writes that "the battlefield is symbolic of the field of life." The heroine does not go into battle but instead uses fortitude, patience, perseverance, imagination, craftiness, and stamina on her journey. There are no weapons of destruction for the true heroine's journey; none are needed. She looks within herself and decides what is needed in each moment. The female's journey is about integration of the self, which had long been ignored.

The story of Medusa is an example of a female knowing what she needs, finding the means to achieve the goal, and integrating it. This is one of my favorite stories, and I use Valerie Estelle Frankel's version of the tale from her book *From Girl to Goddess: The Heroine's Journey through Myth and Legend*.

The young, beautiful, motherless maiden Athena was born from the head of Zeus. Raised by her father, she is forever the virgin and is closely tied to him. She has her spear, shield, and breastplate, which she uses to fight in battles. One day, Athena goes home to her temple and finds Poseidon raping the beautiful young maiden Medusa. Traumatized, Athena turns in horror at the sight and the knowledge of what is happening to young Medusa. She thinks that Medusa has no protection from this type of treatment, so she waves her spear to make Medusa so ugly that anyone who dares look at her will turn to stone. For protection, Medusa's head is covered with snakes so she can see in all directions at all times. Athena then banishes Medusa to the underworld, where she will be safe. Athena does this to protect Medusa from future rapes, but unknowingly, she has also cut Medusa off from not only the divine sexual mysteries of the priestess but from her own self, as well. Athena then dismisses the incident and continues to be daddy's little girl and a sexless champion of the patriarchy. Medusa lives in the underworld, as feminine power raped by male authority.

At this point in the tale, Athena's younger brother, Perseus, is trying to save his mother from the patriarchal dominance of King Polydectes. To keep Perseus occupied and out of the way, the king orders him to obtain the head of Medusa. Perseus prays to Athena, and hearing her brother's cry for help, Athena decides to help Perseus while also helping herself.

Perseus needs the patriarchal rage of Medusa, and Athena now knows she needs to bring back this feminine side of herself to become a whole goddess. Athena equips

Perseus with all the feminine regalia that he will need to enter into the underground of the feminine realm: winged sandals, a mirrored shield with which to gaze at Medusa, an invisibility helmet, and a magic pouch. The only thing that Perseus has that is not symbolically feminine is his sword, which he uses to obtain the head of Medusa. Although Perseus is on his own hero's journey, Athena is using him as a pawn to fulfill her own psychological needs.

Medusa allows Perseus into the underworld, knowing he, too, is a victim of the patriarchy. Perseus slices off her head, which sets her free, as she is no longer frozen in the memory of the past and is able to return to the living. Medusa's children, Pegasus and Chrysaor, are released to the living, as well. Perseus brings the head of Medusa to Athena. She incorporates the head into her breastplate and takes back the invisibility helmet. These symbols, along with freeing Medusa, allow Athena to regain all the feminine wisdom and knowledge of the underground, which she had pushed deep within herself long ago. She has become a whole goddess at last. Her heroine's journey is complete.

The telling of this story is important to explain integration for the female psyche but also to demonstrate the importance of telling a story from the feminine perspective. The story of Athena, Medusa, and Perseus shifts when told from the heroine Athena's point of view instead of the hero Perseus. The films that come out of Hollywood are predominantly told from the masculine point of view. In fact, in 1998 and again in 2007, the top 100 greatest films of all time had only seven films that told their story from the female's point of view. This is more than tragic. Women represent 51 percent of the population, and not telling stories from their point of view means the perspective of more than half of the population is not being shown. There are many films that have strong female characters or leading ladies, yet regardless of how strong a role they play, their stories are being told from the male protagonist's point of view.

Having women's perspectives recognized is as important on screen as it is off screen. According to Anneke Smelik, author of *And the Mirror Cracked*, the demand for authentic female recognition in films is strong. She writes that "female spectators want to be able to identify with lifelike heroines without having to be annoyed by sexist clichés or transported by hyperbolical stereotypes."

Be aware of whose perspective you use when telling your story. Hopefully, you noted how Athena did not have to go anywhere to accomplish her journey. The boon for the heroine is nonexistent; instead, her journey is about integrating the transformation she goes through.

In chapter 11, we will discuss the patriarchal taint that many fairy tales have and what it means as a storyteller of the feminine. Where do we look for a new perspective?

We live in a world where it is hard to imagine a society without patriarchy, but the study of Indigenous cultures in the past can offer glimpses of this kind of world.

—Kim Anderson, Life Stages and Native American Women

Making Changes – We Don't Need Rescued, Thank You Very Much

As you have read so far, there are many female myths to help guide women through life transformations; however, fairy tales dominate for the heroine's journey. These tales are concerned with the individual and the transformation that is undertaken at the moment. Fairy tales do not reflect large cultural events the way myths do. Women's journeys are transformative in nature, and fairy tales help guide these transformations. All of these tales began as the oral telling of stories handed down from female to female as teaching tools. They were always told from the female point of view and would include language and symbolism that only women would relate to. Again, everything in fairy tales is symbolic; nothing is trivial. Fairy tales are about growth and transformation because, unlike the hero's journey, which is all about conquest, the female's journey is about saving the family and transformation.

Sadly, most of today's common literary fairy tales are Eurocentric in nature and were re-written by men in the late 1600s. This led to tales being told from the male perspective of what a woman should be rather than the true feminine nature of a female. We are led to believe that the fairy tale is pure, but as Frank Zipes, the author of numerous books on fairy tales, writes, the fairy tale has been contaminated by social class, Christianity, and patriarchy. Joan Gould, author of *Spinning Straw into Gold*, tells us that the more patriarchal the storyteller or society is, the more victimized and in need of being saved the heroine becomes. The female perspective, which was in place for generations when orally shared tales were passed from mother to daughter, was tarnished once these tales were rewritten by men. The largest collection comes from the Brothers Grimm from Germany; Charles Perrault, from France; and Andrew Lang, from England, over a two-hundred-year period. The perspectives of many of the oral tales began to change. What were once tales about and for women began to take on the air of the patriarchy.

One of the most poignant examples of the patriarchal influence in changing a story is the tale of Rumpelstiltskin. In the most common version of this tale, re-written by the Brothers Grimm in 1857, a father bargains away his daughter by telling the king that she can spin straw into gold. The king brings the maiden to his castle, locks her in a room filled with straw, and tells her she must spin all the straw into gold by morning or she will be killed. When the maiden is not able to achieve this feat, a small, peculiar man magically enters the locked room and tells her he will do the spinning—for a price. She gives him her necklace as payment. In the morning, the king sees all the gold thread. Excited, he places the heroine into a larger room filled with even more straw, expecting more gold thread by morning. That night, the small man returns, and the maiden gives him her ring in payment for more spinning. The next day, the scenario is repeated. But that night, when the small man appears, the maiden has nothing more to give to him, so she promises him her firstborn, and the peculiar man spins the straw into gold once again.

The king then marries the maiden. The new queen gives birth to a son a year later. The small, peculiar man, whose name is Rumpelstiltskin, shows up to collect his payment and take her son from her. She pleads with him, and he finally strikes a new bargain. If she can guess his name within three days, she can keep her son. On the first two nights, she cannot guess his name. On the third day, the queen sends a male messenger into the forest to spy on the little man. The spy overhears Rumpelstiltskin saying his own name. That night, when Rumpelstiltskin comes to the queen, she knows his name, and she is able to keep her son.

The original tale of Rumpelstiltskin was orally told to Jacob Grimm in 1808 and recorded in 1810. The oral tale was quite different from what was finally published in 1857. The original female tale is much shorter and is told from the heroine's point of view. A synopsis is given here.

There once was a maiden who could spin gold thread but could not produce yarn. She was sad and sat on the roof and began to cry. A tiny man appeared and said he would tell her future to help her out of her troubles, but she must promise to give him her firstborn child. The young maid promised him, and he told her that a young prince would come and take her to his castle, where they would be married. He left, and sure enough, the future he foretold happened, and after one year, the princess gave birth to a baby boy.

The tiny man reappeared, ready to take the child. She begged and pleaded and said he could have anything he wanted other than the child, but he would accept nothing else. Finally, the tiny man reconsidered, and he gave her three days to guess his name. If she could not, the child would be his.

The princess thought about it for two days but could not come up with his name. On the third day, she sent one of her faithful maids into the forest the tiny man had come from. While the maid was hiding, she saw the tiny man riding around a fire on a cooking ladle, singing, "If only the princess knew my name was Rumpelstiltskin." The maid rushed back to the princess and told her everything.

The tiny man appeared at midnight, ready to take the child. The princess guessed many names, then she finally said, "Is your name Rumpelstiltskin?" When the tiny man heard this, he was furious. He said, "The devil must have told you," and he flew out the window on his cooking ladle.

The differences between these two stories are not subtle, especially the patriarchal viewpoint in the Brothers

Grimm version. In the oral story from 1810, there is no father bargaining his daughter away or king threatening her with death. The young maiden's problem is her own. She cannot spin thread or yarn, only gold. Yarn and thread are needed for her to earn a living making clothing and other items. When Rumpelstiltskin appears, there is no spinning done by the little man, only negotiation with the young maiden. Once the maiden becomes a princess and has a child, Rumpelstiltskin comes to collect on the deal, and they renegotiate the terms together. The princess requests the aid of another female to help her, and when the princess tells the little man his name, he flies away on the feminine symbol of a cooking ladle. The entire tale is filled with feminine symbolism and is supportive of the heroine—the power she holds and the decisions she makes for herself. The original oral tale describes a young maiden transforming into a powerful woman and shrewd mother who under no circumstances will be forced to give up her child. She is not a victim of her father, a king, or Rumpelstiltskin. This telling is a true heroine's journey. When researching tales, always look for those where the heroine holds her own power. They will be a truer version.

Many of the tales common to Eurocentric literature have this patriarchal bias. According to Marie-Louise von Franz, the problem with the fairy tale is that the male authors project what Jung calls the "anima." This is the portion of the male psyche that has feminine characteristics. Feminine figures in the tales can be the male's anima projection or what he thinks a woman should be, and not necessary what a woman thinks she should be. The specific characteristics that are emphasized are influenced by the sex of the person who last wrote the tale.

Western women seem to struggle to find a true feminine figure to identify with, and von Franz writes that Jung believed this is because women have no representation in the Christian religion. There is Eve, and there is Mother Mary, but they each project only one side of the feminine. Von Franz writes in *Feminine in Fairy Tales* that in societies that are matrifocal, "women have natural confidence in their own womanhood. They know their importance and that they are different from men in a special way, and that this does not imply any inferiority. Therefore, they can assert their human existence and being in a natural way." If one hunts long and deep enough, tales can be found that retain signs of tales told long before the written versions.

In tales where women support women, one can make the assumption that the patriarchy is not very involved. The inclusion of sisters in female stories is one sign of older oral tales and the age-old feminine wisdom. We see patriarchal bias in the transition of the original tale of Sleeping Beauty from the maiden waking on her own, when her inner transformation is complete, to the tale written one hundred years later, in which the prince rescues the maiden with his kiss. The tale of *Beauty and the Beast* has definitive signs of a patriarchal influence, although the literary tale was written by a woman in 1756. This story of initiation reflected what women went through during that time period—exchanging one dominant man for another—so there was enormous value in having a story that helped guide them through the process.

When using fairy tales and female myths for story creation or filmmaking, one must be aware of the male's inappropriate anima projection and patriarchal influences so as not to perpetuate the patriarchy. Knowing female psychology and what true feminine symbolism is and what it means can be very helpful in creating films about women that are authentic. Look for the power the heroine holds. Is she being rescued? If so, dig deeper, and find the version where she rescues herself. Is she passive, or is she using one of the metaphorical chrysalis times to help her integrate? If a tale has eliminated the mentorship of the heroine's sisters, please do not use it. Unless, of course, you adapt the sisters back in.

The question now becomes, is there a place to look for tales that don't have a patriarchal bias? We have learned that tales from Great Mother societies are all but gone. There are remnants left, though, and we now know what to look for. But are there tales that represent the feminine in cultures that are nonpatriarchal? I believe the indigenous cultures of the world can lead us to beautiful stories about the female when she was strong and accepted for the many facets of her being. Are there stories remaining from these equity-based societies?

Before colonization, most of the numerous tribes in North America were structured as matrilineal. Laura Klein and Lillian Ackerman write in *Women and Power in Native North America* that "there was a uniform theme . . . of balanced reciprocity" and that "the worlds of men and women were, and are, distinctly different but not perceived as hierarchical." Although tribes had different creation stories and various forms of societal structures, there were not many that were patriarchal. With these types of societal structures, one could easily assume that the stories mothers and grandmothers told to young girls were based on values different from stories created in a patriarchal society. The genocide and forced assimilation of Native Americans by the European colonizers caused many of these stories to be lost, along with languages and cultural intricacies. However, tribal systems have been operating for thousands of years, and colonization will not undo them.

Dr. Cutcha Risling Baldy, a professor of Native American Studies at Humboldt State University, states that many of the stories about the life transformations women go through still remain with the tribes. The ceremonies practiced long before colonization took place are beginning to become part of their lives once again. She states that one of the large differences that still exist between Native and Eurocentric cultures is their perception of menstruation. Before colonization, all Native cultures celebrated the beginning of menstruation—and not just the women celebrated, but the entire community. These ceremonies are finding their way back into the Native communities, creating a sense of empowerment and acceptance of womanhood for the young girls who participate. A beautiful film about the Dine culture that depicts these ceremonies is *Drunktown's Finest*. The current Eurocentric culture still has taboos about menstruation, and there are not many tales that reflect the beauty of this time in the lives of females.

We began this chapter discussing the patriarchal bias many tales took after they were re-written by men such as the Brothers Grimm, Perrault, and others. When adapting these tales for film, storytellers must be diligent to ensure that the patriarchal taint is removed. If it is not, we perpetuate the patriarchy. I believe that the stories about women coming from equity-based societies, such as those of the many Native American cultures, can help eliminate the existing patriarchal tales. There is a surge of Native American films being made that give us a glimpse into equity-based cultures. *Atanarjuat, The Fast Runner* tells an old tale in which harmony is of the utmost importance. *Before Tomorrow* is the story of a wise-woman heroine who makes life-and-death decisions for her grandson's life as well as her own. *Drunktown's Finest* gives a glimpse into the Dine culture through the coming-of-age ceremony for a young girl.

In chapter 12, all the important element of the heroine's journey are brought together for you.

Turns out that the fabled Hero's Journey is a bunch of hooey when you're writing about Heroines.

—Jill Soloway, Los Angeles Magazine

So… What Did I Just Say? – Let's Summarize

We have questioned the gender of Joseph Campbell's monomyth as described in his 1949 book *A Hero with a Thousand Faces*. Campbell argued that there was no difference between the mythical journey of the hero and the heroine. However, we have seen that the reasons why the two take their journeys, how they achieve their goals, and what those ultimate goals are differ greatly. They differ enough that to say the two journeys are the same immensely devalues the journey of the heroine.

The following summary highlights the most important elements that distinguish a female's journey from her masculine counterpart.

The heroine will take an adventure for only two reasons: to save or help the family in one way or another, or to go through a transformative time in her life. The masculine hero wants a quest. He wants to get out into the world and slay its many dragons. The heroine may never leave home to accomplish her goals. Family is at home, and family is of utmost importance to her. She will do whatever it takes to protect them. As previously stated, there are more sisters who save brothers and daughters who save fathers than the other way around.

The heroine is a transformer. She transforms herself as well as those around her. The hero makes one transformation in his life, from boy to man. The heroine transforms from girl to woman, from woman to mother, and from mother to wise woman. These heroic journeys are important and are told in beautiful tales thousands of years old.

The heroine seldom uses violence to accomplish her goals. She does not need to be clad in armor and wield a sword to transform or to save family. She is cunning, uses her intuition, has her mentor's guidance, and knows exactly what to do and when. Our heroine does not falter in her journey. Her instincts are too great for second-guessing. If she is ever in need of a weapon, it will usually be of a long-distance type.

Being still can be very powerful for the heroine. Females hold an immense amount of power when they are still. This stillness can come in many forms, from deep sleep to quietly weaving or spinning. She is not being passive in any sense of the word.

The heroine's mentors are always feminine. She has a plethora of supporting mentors for her journey. At times, they are in the form of animals and birds, who bring guidance and support. Every heroine has a fairy godmother who bestows wisdom and various items for her journey. The evil stepmother or wicked witch plays an important role in teaching the heroine about transformation and what lies ahead on the road of life. Finally, there are the heroine's metaphorical sisters. They are extremely important to the heroine and play an integral part in her journey; sisterhood is powerful and gives all sorts of needed insight to the heroine.

The heroine cannot master the mother as the hero masters the father. We discussed female psychological principles as they relate to Freud's Oedipal complex. The female holds the mother figure as all the good there is in the world, and one does not conquer good. The heroine will one day become the mother. There are no tales that represent the daughter conquering the mother.

Integration is critical for the heroine. We discussed numerous tales showing how the female integrates the power and wisdom that she has suppressed because of thousands of years of patriarchal rule. The heroine's journey shows her the duality within herself and the mandatory acknowledgment and acceptance of this; she holds her own power over her own life.

We also discussed whether the female tales used to describe the heroine's journey have a patriarchal bias to them. We found that numerous modern-day female fairy tales were written by men, creating a masculine as well as a patriarchal bias. We explored Jungian psychologist and fairy tale scholar Marie-Louise von Franz's view that Western women themselves may not have a true sense of what the feminine actually is. Eurocentric women have been inundated by stories that describe women coming from the man's anima projection. When creating films, it is imperative that a strong knowledge of female psychology and perspective is used.

We discussed where to look for female stories that are not biased by the patriarchy. We saw archaeologically that there were societies some 3,500 years ago, termed "Great Mother" societies, that were not patriarchal in structure but equity-based and matrifocal. However, the stories from this time are long gone, yet if one looks long and deep enough, tales can be found that resemble this gynocentric time. We discussed how Native American culture pre-contact were also equity-based societies. Research into the plethora of female stories from these many indigenous cultures could be a gold mine for stories that do not reflect the patriarchy. However, when researching these stories, remember to view them through the indigenous culture's eyes to avoid seeing them through a Eurocentric lens.

I hope these many elements of the heroine's journey have opened your eyes and given you a new perspective when viewing and creating films. Symbolism is very important to the psyche, so use it wisely. Just as in tales, nothing is trivial in film. Old stories about courageous heroines need to be brought to the forefront to guide the next generation of young girls. New films must be created that show the empowered young maiden who uses her ingenuity and resourcefulness to find her way in the world, to find the prince or princess of *her* choosing, create the family that *she* wants, as she goes from one adventure to the next—as she did, "Once Upon a Time..."

Anyone in the media has a very large megaphone that can reach a lot of different people, and so ... whatever they produce has an influence and is teaching somebody something.

—George Lucas, *The Mythology of Star Wars*

Chapter 13

And It's a Wrap...

Well, there you have it: The Heroine's Journey. I wrote this book hoping that it would answer questions concerning writing female characters that other females can psychologically relate to, to create films that will make a difference in how one views the journey of the feminine, to give validation to this sacred journey instead of allowing the patriarchy to minimize it. If the information helps you, I would love to hear from you. I am always open to reading scripts and consulting on projects. Please give me your input so we can add to the heroine's journey and hopefully make it as commonplace at that of the hero's journey.

I also wrote this book to bring awareness to the importance of fairy tales in the psychological journey of the feminine. Joseph Campbell gave us an amazing book for the psychological journey of the masculine, but because of his patriarchal lens, he did not make the distinction for the feminine psyche. It's time we become aware of it and get stories into the public eye through the use of film that represents the female's perception within the feminine journey.

You now know there *is* a difference between the hero's journey and the heroine's journey and what those differences are. It's time to write scripts about badass ladies that complete their journey without ever using violence. The young ones and their mothers will forever be in your debt.

You will no longer have a negative thing to say about the evil stepmother and wicked witch, knowing that she represents what every good mother becomes when her daughter is in high school. You also know that she will return to all the good that her daughter wants for herself. You will now hold the feminine sacred as you never have before.

This book is *your* fairy godmother, with a bit of wicked witch added to give you the push you need to make changes in the stories we hear, read, and see. Now, get on out there and create heroic journeys of the feminine that you know other women will *finally* be able to relate to. You got this...

Film is no longer seen as reflecting meanings, but as constructing them; thus cinema as a cultural practice actively produces meaning about women and femininity.

—Anneke Smelik, And the Mirror Cracked

Chapter 14

Extra! Extra!
No Sexy Heroine Here;
She's Real

In this bonus chapter, I analyze four films to see what elements of the heroine's journey they contain, if any. The chosen films relate directly to the many elements of the heroine's journey discussed in the previous chapters. The films meet specific categories: a film that specifically represents a heroine taking her adventure because of family; a film that represents a transformative time in the heroine's life; and a film that represents a female in Campbell's classic hero's journey. The general population's familiarity with the chosen films was important but not crucial in my selection. The films chosen are:

Beauty and the Beast

This film was selected to represent the heroine's journey to find her mythological other and her transformation from maiden to woman. The tale was created from the original literary tale of Eros and Psyche, which we discussed in detail in chapter 8. The analysis includes a comparison between Eros and Psyche and the original tale of Beauty and the Beast to demonstrate how Hollywood, and Disney in particular, adapt tales using patriarchal bias. I analyzed the live action film of *Beauty and the Beast* created by Disney and released in 2017.

The Wizard of Oz

This film shows how important home and family are to a heroine. It shows the important lessons the heroine always needs to have on her journey through life, while telling the story of a young woman's transformation from maiden to woman without a prince being involved. Dorothy's integration of important values about herself are beautifully portrayed. Additionally, it is on the American Film Institute's top 100 films of all time and is familiar to much of the public.

Moana

Although this film features a young heroine, it depicts the integration part of the heroine's journey. The film is based on the numerous Polynesian cultures that are historically matrilineal. It references the goddess mythology and equity-based cultures discussed in chapter 11. An actual mythological figure, the demigod Maui, shares the action with the young heroine. However, this film is not entirely a heroine's journey. Hollywood just can't get away from placing a heroine in the masculine journey of the hero.

Star Wars: Episode VII – The Force Awakens

This film was chosen because it features a female protagonist taking Campbell's masculine journey of the hero. In addition, the six previous Star Wars films were created by George Lucas, who has acknowledged that Campbell's work greatly influenced the creation of his films. This film, although created by Disney and not Lucas, is a typical representation of the hero's journey.

Let's look at an analysis of each film and its relation to the heroine's journey.

Beauty and the Beast

Can anyone truly be happy if they're not free?

Beauty and the Beast begins with the introduction of the prince and his struggles. The film becomes more about the Beast and his need to become a prince again rather than focusing on Belle and her transformation. Disney also leaves out the role of Belle's sisters, who we now know are so important to a young heroine.

This tale is widely known, so let's dive right into the heroine themes. Belle's mother is missing in her life, which is common in most beast marriage tales. The father is the key figure because the heroine is giving up one dominant man for another.

Belle's father goes missing, and when she realizes he's gone, she goes out to look for him. This is a perfect representation of the heroine doing whatever is necessary to save her family. Belle arrives at the castle, where she believes her father is being held captive. Here she finds talking pieces of furniture, who wonder if Belle could be the chosen one. The "chosen one" theme is not portrayed in any of the old Beauty and the Beast tales. This is more about destiny and the hero's journey. Disney has made this adaptation to be more about the Beast and *his need* to transform than Belle's transformation from a maiden to a woman. Belle finds her father trapped in a cell and trades places with him to protect him. The Beast is surprised by this act of love.

The talking pieces of furniture get her out of the cell and into a room. They tell her she has run of the castle except for one room. This is representational of all the beast tales. There is a place, a room, or someone (as in Eros and Psyche) that must not be looked at. It is forbidden to the maiden, but as she grows up, the forbidden area becomes intriguing, and she must look into it. This is the part where her sisters would usually play their important role; they would push her into looking in the room. Disney does not include the sisters in this tale, so symbolically, no one with female knowledge to share is there for Belle as she transitions into womanhood.

Belle tries to escape from the castle but gets caught by the Beast. He storms out of the room and goes to the forbidden room, where there is a single rose that is losing its petals. Once all the petals have fallen, he will have no chance of becoming a prince again. The film continues to focus more and more on the Beast and what he needs from Belle; she is just a means to an end for him. The film depicts the Beast desiring his own transformation, which is not what the original tale is about. That tale is about Belle's transformation coming about while she transforms the Beast into the prince she desires.

Belle becomes intrigued by the forbidden room and enters it. The Beast catches her and screams at her to go. She runs out of the castle and jumps onto her horse to gallop home, but wolves surround her, and the Beast rescues her. He is attacked during the skirmish, and Belle gets him back to the castle and nurses his wounds.

During the time that Belle takes care of the Beast, she questions her choices. This symbolizes the young maiden growing up. She is wiser now. This is part of the heroine's journey. Should she choose to go running home to Daddy and live the life of a little girl, or stay and become the mistress of her own castle? In most beast tales, the heroine goes back to the family—usually her sisters—or the family comes to her. In this rendition by Disney, Belle only sings about family. All the time that Belle and the Beast spend together is symbolic of Belle metaphorically taming her beast.

In time, the Beast realizes that Belle must go to her father to make sure he is okay. He gives her a mirror (symbolically female) so she has a way to look back on him and her time at the castle. The Beast has made a sacrifice for love. The story has returned its focus to his transformation.

When Belle gets to her father, she sees that he has been taken prisoner because of his crazy talk about a beast in a castle. Using her mirror, Belle shows the crowd the Beast. The leader of the group is the man who wants Belle to be his wife, but she has always refused him. He rouses up the crowd and says they must go kill the beast.

At the end of the film, there is a fight between the talking furniture and the townspeople. The Beast is once again injured, and Belle runs to him and tells him how much she loves him. This breaks the spell, and the Beast becomes the handsome prince he once was, but this time he has love in his heart.

Parts of the film depict the true heroine's journey. The Beast represents the heroine's future. Because of the history of arranged marriages, the maiden's future husband may seem like a beast to her. However, in all of these tales, the heroine has the choice of whether to stay with the beast and transform him or go back to her family. The heroine's transformation of the beast into her metaphorical prince is representative of her own transformation from an innocent maiden into a woman ready to run her own castle. The filmmakers at Disney adapted this tale using a masculine lens, so it became about the Beast's tale as much as or more so than it did Belle's transformation.

There is no additional man in any of the literary tales about beast marriages. There is no violence. The saving of the beast is part of the heroine's journey, though not in Disney's format. The heroine will do whatever is necessary to save family. Once the maiden has decided that this is the man for her, she will do what it takes to make sure he is safe, and spells are broken. *She* holds the power to transform her beast into her prince.

The Wizard of Oz

You've always had the power.

The Wizard of Oz opens with Dorothy being frustrated with her Auntie Em and Uncle Henry because they won't listen to her about the neighbor lady, Miss Almira Gulch, who is mean to Dorothy's dog, Toto. As is typical in most fairy tales, Dorothy's parental figures are not her mother and father. Toto represents Dorothy's family, whom she will do anything to protect. Auntie Em and Uncle Henry are dealing with baby chicks and can't be bothered with Dorothy. She goes to the three farm hands to see if they will listen to her. One tells her to be brave and one tells her to be smart when dealing with Miss Gulch. These characters are set up as the heroine's symbolic instinct and intuition to help her with her journey. It is unusual for a heroine's journey that they are men.

Dorothy falls into the pen with the hogs, and Auntie Em tells her to go somewhere where she won't get into trouble. Dorothy wonders if there is such a place. She sings "Somewhere Over the Rainbow." This song sets up her journey to the "other world," the land of the female's unconscious.

The wicked witch is introduced in the form of Miss Almira Gulch, the mean old lady who wants to take Toto away from Dorothy. Miss Gulch has orders from the sheriff, and Auntie Em and Uncle Henry can't help Dorothy. Miss Gulch takes the dog away, and Dorothy runs into her bedroom, crying. However, little Toto escapes and runs back to Dorothy. She believes that her only option to save

Toto is to run away, so she packs her bag, and off she goes down the road. To Dorothy, Toto is family, and she is willing to take any type of adventure to save her little dog.

Along the road, she meets Professor Marvel, who shows her a crystal ball. This represents the magic that Dorothy thinks she needs; she is looking outside herself for answers. The professor tells her that there is an older woman looking for her. The woman is crying and distraught. This makes Dorothy think of Auntie Em, so she changes her mind about running away and hurries back home. This scene plants the seed that she must go home later in the story. Home and family are important to the heroine.

A terrible storm is coming, and everyone on the farm goes into the shelter. Dorothy makes it back home, but she can't find anyone. She is on her bed in her bedroom when her window is knocked off by the wind and hits her on the head. She falls back onto the bed, unconscious. This is the metaphorical deep-sleep chrysalis that many maidens go through and which we discussed in chapter 6. While she is knocked out, Dorothy has a dream, which signifies her journey through the unconscious. This allows her the time to grow, mature, and ultimately, realize what is important to her.

Dorothy wakes up while the house is turning and spinning. It hits the ground with a jolt. When she steps outside, the colors in this new land make her realize that she is no longer in Kansas. A bubble comes down from the sky, growing larger and larger. A beautiful lady appears from the bubble and asks Dorothy if she is a good witch or a bad witch. This is Dorothy's fairy godmother, or the "good mother," who lovingly shows up at the perfect time to give the heroine exactly what she needs. Dorothy answers that she is neither, but Glinda, the Good Witch of the North, shows her how the house fell right on top of the bad Witch of the East and killed her. Notice that Dorothy herself didn't kill the Wicked Witch of the East; the house, which is symbolically female, killed her. Dorothy herself used no violence and had no intention of hurting anyone. She started on this adventure to take care of her little dog, Toto, not to kill bad witches. That would be a hero's journey.

All the little people from Munchkinland come out to pay tribute to the heroine Dorothy, who killed the witch who had held them hostage. Ding dong, the witch is dead! The Wicked Witch of the West appears, asking who killed her sister. The Wicked Witch of the West represents the "bad mother," who forces the heroine to transform and grow up. In the literary tale, the witch makes Dorothy wash floors and take care of the castle.

The ruby slippers that the Wicked Witch of the East had been wearing magically transfer to Dorothy's feet. The Wicked Witch of the West tries to take them, but she can't. The Good Witch of the North tells Dorothy to keep them on no matter what, because their magic must be powerful. The ruby slippers represent the role Dorothy has stepped into. They are her power—not a sword, but shoes. This is a beautiful representation of the heroine's journey, much like Cinderella and the glass slippers. Dorothy doesn't yet realize the power she holds.

Glinda tells Dorothy to leave Oz because she has made an enemy of the Wicked Witch of the West. She tells her to go back to where she is safe, as she is not yet ready to be out on her own. Glinda says there are things Dorothy needs to learn. Dorothy asks Glinda how she will get home if she can't use the house to get there. Glinda tells her to go see the powerful Wizard of Oz, who lives in the Emerald City, and ask him how to get home. This represents Dorothy looking outside herself for answers and guidance. The Wizard represents the strong father (patriarchy) who will stand up for the heroine and give her what she needs, which Uncle Henry had failed to do.

Dorothy doesn't yet think she is capable of knowing and doing on her own. To get to Oz, all Dorothy has to do is "follow the Yellow Brick Road." The Yellow Brick Road represents the road between the heroine's conscious and unconscious mind. The journey represents her bringing her unconscious and conscious together and realizing the power she holds: her own voice of authority. This is integration.

Dorothy sets out on the Yellow Brick Road. She comes to a crossroad and meets Scarecrow, who is in need of a brain. Dorothy asks if he would like to join her on her journey to Oz. He could then ask the Great Wizard to give him a brain. Scarecrow represents Dorothy's instinctual knowledge. The two become a team; collaboration is a feminine trait. They are not going to conquer anything or anyone, they are just going to ask the Wizard for help.

Dorothy and Scarecrow find themselves in a grove of talking apple trees. As we know, the red apple is symbolically feminine. Eve eats the apple of knowledge and loses her innocence; Snow White eats the poisoned apple and loses consciousness.

Dorothy and Scarecrow find Tin Man, who is looking for a heart. They encourage him to join them on their way to the Emerald City to ask the Wizard for help. The team now heads farther into the dark forest. Remember, the dark forest is a feminine place. Tin Man represents Dorothy's own desire to lead from her heart, as she is kind and compassionate.

The group meets the Cowardly Lion, who is looking for courage. He, too, joins the team going to find the Wizard of Oz. Dorothy tells him that the Wizard will fix everything. The Cowardly Lion represents Dorothy's own courage, which she must learn to use. Trusting in the Wizard to get her home symbolizes Dorothy's continued search outside of herself for her power—for the patriarchal father/God to save the day. Dorothy wants to go home, and the Wizard will be the one to get her there.

All of the scenes in which Dorothy meets and gathers her team introduce the heroine's instinctual knowledge. Snow White has her seven dwarves, Psyche has her ants and birds, and Cinderella has her many mice, all of which are symbolically the heroine's own intuition.

Dorothy and her friends finally arrive at the Emerald City. They are allowed in because Dorothy is wearing the ruby slippers. When they go to see the Wizard, the doorman tells them that they can't come in. Dorothy cries, and he lets them in.

The Great Wizard tells them he will grant their requests, but first they must bring back the broomstick of the Wicked Witch of the West. The heroine is tested in many ways but also receives help with her trials. She must resist pity and have willpower and fortitude. This is the sacrifice that many tales show heroines going through. The hero is usually tested through physical demands. Dorothy is not asked to perform any acts of violence. She is instructed to just bring back the Wicked Witch of the West's broom, not to kill her.

The group goes into the haunted forest. They think they see birds, but they are flying monkeys that the Wicked Witch has sent to capture Dorothy and Toto and bring them to her. Inside her castle, the Wicked Witch takes Toto and places him in a basket. The Witch says that if Dorothy wants to keep her dog, she must relinquish the ruby slippers. The Witch again tries to take the slippers from Dorothy's feet but realizes that they won't come off as long as Dorothy is alive. The Witch turns the hourglass, filled with red sand, and says that when it runs out, Dorothy will die.

Toto jumps from the basket and escapes. He runs back to the forest to find Tin Man, Scarecrow, and Lion. They set off to rescue Dorothy. The group breaks into the Witch's castle and finds where Dorothy is hidden. Tin Man chops the door apart just as the hourglass expires. They all run to escape, but the Witch corners them and says she will kill the three companions and then Dorothy. She uses her broom to get fire from a torch and sets Scarecrow on fire. Dorothy tries to save Scarecrow by throwing a bucket of water on him. Some of the water hits the Wicked Witch of the West and melts her, killing her. Everyone is joyous. Dorothy's intention was not to kill the Witch but to save Scarecrow. Both the bucket and the water are symbolically feminine. Water removes all evil, including a wicked witch!

Dorothy and her friends take the broom back to the Wizard so their wishes can be granted. The Wizard tells them to come back the next day. Toto opens up a curtain, exposing the man who is acting as the Wizard. Caught, the man confesses, saying he is a good man, just a bad wizard. He bestows knowledge and wisdom upon Scarecrow, courage to the Cowardly Lion, and a heart to Tin Man. He tells Dorothy that he will take her back to Kansas himself, in a hot air balloon.

Dorothy, Toto, and the Wizard get into the balloon and are ready to take off. Toto sees a cat and jumps out. Dorothy gets out and runs after Toto, and the balloon goes up without her. She is heartbroken, thinking she will never get back to Kansas and her family. Glinda, the Good Witch of the North, arrives in her bubble. She tells Dorothy that she has had the power to get home all along, she just had to learn it for herself.

Dorothy wakes up in her own bed back at the farm in Kansas, mumbling, "There's no place like home." She tries to tell everyone about the land of Oz, but no one listens. She is just glad to be home.

The final scene sees the heroine where she started, but now she knows much more than when she began her journey. The young heroine starts her journey to save family and then reunites with them. All heroines feel they have accomplished their journey once family is restored. This film is about the attributes and importance of home. It shows the transformation a young maiden must go through to be able to take the next steps in life. This journey is also for the heroine to see that she has her own power, to understand that she does not need to look outside herself, because the answers she is looking for are all inside of her.

Moana

One day, who knows how far I'll go.

Moana starts with Gramma, an old woman, telling the tale of the demigod Maui as various pictures of Maui's story are shown on the screen. Gramma is telling the story to a group of diapered little toddlers. All are scared to death except one: Moana. Moana's father, the chief, enters to stop Gramma. He makes the point that *no one* goes outside the reef; they are safe here. There are no monsters outside the reef, just rough seas and storms. Gramma insists that sooner or later, someone will have to go.

Baby Moana is toddling down to the beach and toward the ocean. She sees a beautiful seashell that draws her into the ocean. The ocean then parts for her and entices her in with the seashell. As she picks up one seashell, another appears, and so on, luring her into the ocean. The ocean continues to part, allowing her to walk safely on the sand. The ocean shows her a green stone, which represents Te Fiti's heart. She takes it. She hears the voice of her father, and the ocean safely sends her back to the beach. She drops the heart as her father picks her up and tells her not to go into the ocean because it is not safe. He tells her that she will be the next great chief of the village.

Moana's mother enters, picks up Moana, and tells her she will be wonderful. Her father tells her that first she must learn where she is meant to be. This sets up the lesson the story tells. At this point, Moana's journey could be that of either the heroine or the hero, but it is leaning toward the hero's journey because it is Moana's destiny to become the chief. The villagers sing a song that says, "the village is all you need." Moana keeps toddling toward the ocean. Instead of learning to make a basket, she draws pictures of boats.

As Moana grows from a toddler to a young maiden who is still drawn to the ocean, the villagers sing a song about how you must find happiness right where you are. Moana finds Gramma down by the ocean. Gramma encourages Moana to follow the voice inside her. This sets up Gramma as Moana's mentor or subconscious, which is in the realm of the heroine's journey.

Moana is torn between what her family wants her to do and what she wants to do. In *The Wizard of Oz*, Dorothy runs away from home only to keep Toto (family) safe. This is the heroine's journey. At this point in the film, the story is about destiny, which is in the realm of the hero.

Moana's father takes her to the top of a mountain and tells her that when she becomes chief, she will place a stone on top of the others, just as all chiefs before her have done. He tells her that she is the future of the people and that they are not "out there" (he points to the ocean) but "right here" (he points to the village). It is time for her to be who they need her to be. The chief believes there is only one way to be a leader. This may represent how the dominant father suppresses his daughter, pressuring her into doing what he thinks is right for her. This is patriarchal; however, these types of cultures are usually not patriarchal but matrifocal in nature.

The next few scenes show Moana trying to become a leader. The villagers sing a song about "the island gives us what we need, and no one leaves." The message is that Moana can find happiness right where she is.

The next scenes continue to show Moana trying to do what is necessary to become her people's leader. Her two sidekicks, a chicken, Hei Hei, and a little baby pig, Pua, are introduced. In traditional tales, the heroine does not have a sidekick until she needs the wisdom the character represents. Disney has diminished this symbolism in the journey, as Moana's animal pets do not teach or help her in any way.

Trouble begins on the island when the coconuts are spoiled, and fish can no longer be found in the reef. Moana suggests fishing beyond the reef, and her father angrily restates that no one goes beyond the reef, as it is not safe "out there." Moana's mother tells her the story of why Moana's father is so afraid of going beyond the reef. When he was young, he loved the ocean, just as Moana does. He and a buddy took a boat past the reef, and his buddy was killed by the rough seas. She tells Moana that sometimes who we wish we were and what we want to do are just not meant to be.

Moana tries to be a good daughter, but the water calls her. She and her little pig, Pua, take a boat out beyond the reef. She can't maneuver the waves, and they both go overboard. They make it back to the beach, but Pua is now terrified of boats. Gramma finds Moana on the beach. Moana says that her father was right, and she is not going out there anymore. This may be the refusal of the call, but a reason to go on her journey has not yet shown up, just her yearning. Moana decides to go to the mountaintop and put her rock on the pile of stones. Gramma goes into the ocean and plays with the manta rays, saying that when she dies, she wants to come back as one of them.

Gramma and Moana climb a mountain, and Gramma tells Moana that she has been told all the village stories but one. They come to a cave that has been sealed with rocks. Moana moves the rocks. Gramma gives her a torch and tells her to go inside the cave and bang the drum to find out who she really is. Inside the cave, Moana discovers some old boats. One is small enough for her. It has a symbol on the sail that is the same as the one on Te Fiti's heart. It is a feminine symbol. Moana bangs the drum, and a song begins that tells Moana her ancestors were voyagers and discoverers of new islands.

She comes out of the cave and asks Gramma why her ancestors stopped voyaging. Gramma says it was because of Maui. Once Maui stole the heart from Te Fiti, the seas changed, and the voyagers didn't come back. To save their people, the ancestors hid the boats and stayed on the island. But the darkness continued to spread. It took away the fish, draining the life from island after island. Gramma tells Moana that one day, someone will journey across the ocean, find Maui, and take him across the ocean to replace the heart of Te Fiti. She gives Moana the heart that she found when the ocean gave it to her back when she was a little girl. Moana has now become the chosen one. This is the destiny call that is typical of the hero's journey.

Moana interrupts a big village meeting to tell everyone about the hidden boats and how their people used to be voyagers. Her father is furious and goes to burn the boats, but just at that moment, someone tells him that his mother, Gramma, is very ill. They rush to her side. Gramma tells Moana to go—to save the people. At first Moana says no, but she eventually decides to go. She goes home to pack a sack. Her mother is there and helps her; she knows her daughter's destiny. This is the mother-daughter connection, the female knowingness. By leaving, Moana is listening to her grandmother, who is her mentor and fairy godmother. Gramma's dying words are to tell Moana one last time to go to the ocean. There is no greater female symbol than the ocean. Moana boards the smaller boat and sets sail.

The next morning, when she is out on the ocean, Moana realizes that her chicken, Hei Hei, is a stowaway. Although Hei Hei accompanies Moana, the writer's use of the chicken is for jokes only; there is no symbolism given. Hei Hei does not help, guide, or give support to Moana in any way.

That night a storm comes, which symbolizes the hero's crossing of the first threshold, and Moana is washed up on the small sand-and-rock island where Maui lives. This is the ocean-as-mentor putting Moana exactly where she needs to be. Maui sings the song "You're Welcome" for being a demigod. The song describes the story of the Polynesian demigod Maui. Maui then places Moana in a cave and takes off with her boat. His tattoos talk to him, telling him to go back and get the girl. Maui's tattoos are his intuitive sense.

Moana escapes from the cave and dives into the water, right where Maui is getting ready to sail. Maui takes off in her boat without her, but the ocean takes Moana and pops her right onto the boat. Maui throws her off, but the water pops her back on. This reinforces the fact that Moana is the chosen one. It also shows that the ocean is Moana's instinct, or guide and helper, just as Cinderella has her mice and Snow White her birds and bunnies.

The first trial for Maui and Moana is when a boat filled with little coconut people, the Kakamoras, come for them, knowing they have the heart. The bad guys want the heart because they believe they can create life with it. Moana asks Maui to use his magic powers, but he reminds her that he has lost his magic hook. No hook, no magical powers. This loss represents Freud's male castration, which is typical in many films of the hero. This is also the point in the film at which the focus switches to Maui. He is now taking his hero's journey and using Moana as his sidekick.

They get through this trial, but Maui still says he won't go to Te Fiti because they would have to go through an ocean of bad to get there, and there is Ta Kā, the lava monster. Moana convinces Maui to go anyway, because he would then be considered a hero to the world. He agrees, but he has to find his hook first. Finding it is symbolic of gaining his manhood, a reference to Freud again.

They sail to get his fishhook, and Moana asks Maui to teach her to sail. He calls her a princess, to which she says no, she is the daughter of a chief. Maui says if you wear a dress and you have an animal sidekick, you are a princess. This is a dig at the old Disney princesses and bears truth in the heroine's journey. However, in this case, Moana's animal does not help and guide her. This also supports the point that the film has shifted focus to Maui taking his hero's journey. The story is no longer about Moana; she has become merely a sidekick to help Maui on his journey.

Moana and Maui end up on the island where Maui thinks his hook is. Tomatoa, a very large crab, has stolen the hook. Maui tells Moana to stay back, but she climbs the rock right alongside Maui. They enter Lomatai, the realm of monsters, through the top of the mountain. The typical hero's journey includes slaying monsters.

As they climb, Maui tries to understand why Moana's people sent her on this adventure. She tells him that they didn't, the ocean did. Maui makes the comment once again about her being the chosen one. This trope is in the realm of the hero's journey. Moana did not take this adventure to save a family member but for the greater good of saving her people. However, if Moana's village and her people are seen as matrilineal or matrifocal, then it would plausibly be a heroine's journey, as it could be argued that Moana is looking at her entire village as her family. In a Eurocentric culture, family is usually considered blood relations only. From this perspective, Moana's journey out into the world to save the village would then be the hero's journey. If the entire village is considered family in indigenous cultures, one could argue that Moana is actually taking a heroine's journey to save family. It is important to be aware of cultural bias when interpreting and analyzing tales.

Maui opens the top of the mountain and jumps in. Moana follows. They get to the realm of monsters, and another trial takes place. This is all about the hero, Maui, getting his manhood reinstated. Moana helps, but at this point, the journey is not hers. Once Maui gets his hook back, they return to the boat and begin sailing to find Ta Kā. Maui doesn't think they can make it. He believes the adventure is cursed because his shapeshifting ability is not working properly. Moana gives a (feminine) speech about wanting to help Maui; she wants to help him so that he will ultimately help her. This can be interpreted as the heroine using her resourcefulness and wisdom instead of violence to get what she needs for her people.

Maui tells Moana that his parents were human and threw him into the sea because they didn't want him. The gods found him, gave him his hook, and made him Maui, a demigod. But he did everything for the humans, even taking the heart from Te Fiti. This telling is authentic to the Maui myth. The story at this point is still about Maui and his journey. Moana gives Maui a pep talk, and he again wants to defeat Ta Kā. Their next stop is Te Fiti. Maui is now on board with the plan. He continues to help Moana learn sailing and wayfinding. He is now being a mentor to her, teaching her the skills she wants to learn. In the heroine's journey, the role of mentor is usually filled by a female.

They get to the island of Te Fiti. Moana gives Maui the heart and tells him to go save the world. This is typical of the hero's journey. The second trial begins. Maui shapeshifts and flies into the burning volcano entity, Ta Kā. She unleashes her fury on Maui, and Moana tries to get them to a better position. Maui tells her to turn back, but she won't. Ta Kā pushes back, but the ocean pushes them forward. Maui's hook breaks. Maui blames Moana for the problems because she did not turn back. He says that he is nothing without his hook. (Freudian.) Maui leaves Moana.

Moana begins to doubt herself. She tells the ocean to choose someone else, that she is not the right person. This can be interpreted as representing a stereotypical female who can't do anything without a male. There is no room in the heroine's journey for this type of questioning, as the heroine knows what she needs to do to save family. She does not falter. The hero, however, will falter and question, because it is destiny that calls him, not an event. Faltering is a sign of wanting to keep the ego intact.

Moana throws the heart back into the ocean. She sees a fluorescent manta ray (the sign of her grandmother) swim through the boat. The manta ray takes the form of Gramma, who gives Moana a pep talk about knowing who you are. Moana is the chosen one. Again, this is typical for the hero's journey. One can interpret this as the heroine's mentor showing up right when she is needed. It can also be interpreted as the heroine's mentor telling her she has had her power all along, as we see when Glinda the Good Witch tells this to Dorothy. Dorothy waits for the Wizard to help her get home, just as Moana waits for Maui to put the heart back in Te Fiti. This lesson for Moana, as with Dorothy, is about the female knowing she holds her own power in a patriarchally dominated world.

Moana fixes the boat and goes on her way to restore the heart of Te Fiti herself. She needs to get past Ta Kā, who cannot follow her into the ocean. Just as Ta Kā is about to destroy her, Maui flies in. Maui tells Moana, "I got your back, Chosen One. Go save the world." Telling the hero to go out and save the world is something one would hear in a hero's journey. As Maui tries to draw Ta Kā away from Moana, his hook is destroyed; he is castrated one more time.

Moana gets past Ta Kā only to find that Te Fiti is no longer there. A view from above shows she has sunk. Moana turns around to see that Ta Kā is where the heart belongs. Moana takes the heart and holds it high, and Ta Kā sees the heart and stops. Moana walks toward Ta Kā. She tells the ocean to "let her come to me," and the water parts. The ocean parts for Ta Kā, and roaring, Ta Kā heads toward Moana, who is walking on the sand where the ocean parted. A song is sung about Ta Kā: "This is not who you are. You know who you are." The song is also about Moana knowing who she is. Here, Disney Studios had a wonderful opportunity to show that a goddess (Ta Kā) is both the giver and taker of life, the light and the dark, and that both are needed. But the studio chose the patriarchal viewpoint, depicting through song that Ta Kā is the "bad guy" because she has lost her heart. The song conveys that once her heart is returned, she will understand who she really is: the light. The message is that the female should only be the giver of life, the nurturer. Bad song, bad message.

Moana places the heart inside Ta Kā, then Te Fiti rises from the ocean. Ta Kā and Te Fiti are one and the same. Te Fiti takes both Maui and Moana into her grass hands (she is no longer a lava woman). Maui apologizes to Te Fiti for stealing her heart, and she rewards him with a new hook. She rewards Moana with a boat to sail home in. Te Fiti rests once more. Moana and Maui say goodbye. Maui shows Moana his new tattoo depicting Moana in her boat.

Moana returns to her people as a hero and receives big hugs from her mother and father. The father brings out the forbidden boats. Moana places the original pink seashell that drew her to the ocean as a baby on top of the rocks of her ancestors. Finally, Moana and her people voyage across the ocean.

This film provides a good example of the differences between two heroic journeys within one story. Moana is the story's main protagonist, but Maui's journey dominates from the time it starts midway through the film to near the end of the film, when Moana's story returns to dominance.

Disney missed some opportunities to put Moana in a heroine's journey, but it also got a few things right. The ocean and all that it contains have always been symbolically female; the name "Moana" means ocean. Moana is called to the ocean and taken care of by the ocean, which seems right psychologically. Disney dresses Moana in the symbolic colors of female transformation—red, white, and black—when she goes out on her journey. Gramma is Moana's mentor/fairy godmother, and Disney does an exceptional job with her character. She pushes when needed and gives pep talks when they are needed.

What Moana's story is missing is the push from the symbolic bad mother to grow up. The heroine cannot have the light without the dark; they are one and the same, just as with Ta Kā and Te Fiti. In addition, there are no sisters for Moana to receive advice from. With these elements missing, the character could just as easily have been written as a young boy who defies his father. However, like Dorothy and going home in *The Wizard of Oz*, Moana needed to learn that she had the power all along to place the heart back in Ta Kā. She learns to have the courage to listen to her own voice, her own intuition, and not just for the sake of the village but for herself. Maui, just like the Wizard, was truly not needed.

Disney also deserves credit for the representation of Ta Kā and Te Fiti as one and the same entity. This is representational of the divine feminine wisdom that was destroyed under patriarchal rule. There is not a "good goddess" and a "bad goddess"; the female is the ruler of both life and death. But the song that is sung during the scene that shows Ta Kā and Te Fiti as one negates the representation that was just created because it infers that Ta Kā was "bad" and that, by receiving her heart back, she becomes "good" and that this is truly "who she is." That said, Moana has now experienced the duality of life.

Star Wars: Episode VII – The Force Awakens

The belonging you seek is not behind you, it is ahead.

The Force Awakens begins with the little droid BB8 busting in on an older man and a younger man talking about the General (Princess Leia). The old man gives the young man something from a pouch, and suddenly some stormtroopers arrive. The young man tries to get away, but his plane is hit. He places what the old man gave to him inside BB8 and tells the droid to get away. This is reminiscent of Leia putting information inside the droid R2-D2 in Episode IV. BB8 is made of many circles, and the circle is a female talisman. One stormtrooper gets upset when a fellow stormtrooper gets hit; he falters but does not shoot back.

A big, black TIE fighter arrives, and a man in a black mask and black cape (reminiscent of Darth Vader) gets out. The stormtroopers find the old man, and the dark warrior Kylo Ren, dressed in black, asks the old man for the map to get to Luke Skywalker. He kills the old man when he won't divulge the information. The young man, a pilot named Poe, sees this and tries to kill Kylo Ren but is stopped by the force. Poe is taken captive, and his captors kill all the villagers. BB8, who was running away, turns and sees the massive fire. Poe is taken back to the Stormtroopers' base. His hesitant captor, Stormtrooper Finn, is having an anxiety attack. He realizes he can't be a bad guy any more.

On the planet Jakku, a young woman called Rey is scavenging in the desert among all the old plane wreckages. She sells her found items in the marketplace for food. Her attire is sandy-colored with a bit of draping, but overall, it is masculine in appearance. Rey is cooking at home, which is in an abandoned wreckage. She sits outside to eat and hears noise beyond the sand hill above her. She investigates and sees someone trying to capture a small droid (BB8). She rescues the droid, and it stays with her, becoming her sidekick. This represents the Call to Destiny in the hero's journey, just as Luke had his destiny with R2-D2 and C-3PO in Episode IV. Destiny isn't involved in the heroine's journey; instead, the heroine needs to take care of an incident or event regarding family, which propels her into the journey. When this is not the case, the heroine is in a transformative time in her life. Neither of these circumstances fits Rey's experience, so this is a hero's journey so far.

Back on the stormtrooper base, Kylo Ren uses the Force on the captive Poe to retrieve the information about the map to Luke Skywalker. He learns it is hidden inside the droid BB8. Kylo Ren sends Stormtroopers to the planet Jakku to retrieve the droid.

On Jakku, Rey tells BB8 that she is waiting for her family to return to her. This symbolically shows the feminine trait of patience and the importance the heroine puts on family. Rey once again goes to the market to sell her scavenged items. The buyer, seeing the droid, offers Rey a large sum of food rations in exchange for BB8. At first, she agrees, but then she looks down at BB8 and declines. This scene can be interpreted in two ways. First, Rey deciding that the droid needs to stay with her may represent her female intuition, or sense of knowing. Second, the scene may represent the hero's Call to Destiny. Once the two leave the stand, the buyer radios someone to follow her and get the droid.

At the stormtrooper base, Finn, the dissatisfied stormtrooper, decides to help Poe escape. Poe tells him they have to go back to Jakku to retrieve BB8. On the way, their plane is hit, and it crashes on Jakku, knocking Finn unconscious. When he comes to, there is no sign of Poe except for his jacket. Finn takes off his stormtrooper armor and puts on Poe's jacket.

He makes his way to the market area and sees Rey being attacked. He goes to help and then recognizes BB8. Rey comes after him, thinking he wants to steal BB8, like the others. Finn tells her and BB8 that he helped save Poe and that he is a resistance fighter. Rey confers with BB8, and they decide Finn is okay. This is a beautiful depiction of BB8 symbolically representing Rey's own intuition. All heroines have helpers in their journeys who represent their intuition or instinctual nature. In most fairy tales, these helpers are represented by animals who help the heroine during her many tests and trials. It also sets the stage for Finn to become Rey's sidekick, as Han Solo was for Luke in Episode IV. This type of relationship is typical in the hero's journey. The twist in this film is the female-male relationship between hero and sidekick. In Episode IV, Luke did not have a relationship, but his sidekick, Han, did, with Princess Leia. In addition, there has been no mentor established for Rey as yet. This scene is the beginning of the Road of Trials in the hero's journey.

Stormtroopers have landed. They recognize BB8, and a chase ensues. Rey, Finn, and BB8 run for a plane, but it gets blown up just before they get there. They have to go with an old clunker, which is immediately recognizable as the Millennium Falcon from Episode IV. Rey flies the plane while Finn takes the gunner position. A flying chase scene follows as Rey and Finn outmaneuver the stormtroopers and head into space. At this point, Rey's role seems to be made for a hero, not a heroine. There is a gas leak on the plane, and Rey miraculously has the mechanical skills to fix it. Meanwhile, without the crew realizing it, the Falcon gets sucked up into a large ship. As Finn, Rey, and BB8 are hiding in the bottom of the ship, Chewbacca and Han Solo walk in. After a skirmish, a new team is created, and soon they are flying back into space, with Han and Rey at the controls. Han is asked to help them get BB8 to the resistance, and he agrees. They go to the planet Takodana, where Maz Kanata rules.

After they land, Han asks Rey if she would like to join his team. She is flattered, but she knows she needs to get home. This decision puts Rey back into a heroine role; she is concerned about family. Unlike Luke in Episode IV, in which he wanted to leave his family, Rey wants to go back to Jakku to wait for her family.

The crew enters the castle to ask Maz Kanata about a clean ship to get BB8 away. Han knows the dark side has tracked them. Inside the castle is the typical bar scene, reminiscent of Episode IV. The bar is symbolically a masculine arena. When Maz is introduced to the audience, she is the first feminine figure we see in the film. Her large spectacles symbolize feminine perception. In a future episode, she could become Rey's Yoda, not teaching the Force per se, but teaching feminine ways, perception, and intuition. She could be Rey's fairy godmother or mentor figure.

Finn wants to leave and go to the outer rim, and he wants Rey to go with him. This is reminiscent of Han leaving Luke after they rescue Leia. Rey can't believe he wants to leave, so Finn comes clean to Rey about who he really is: a stormtrooper on the run. He leaves, and she stays. Here, Rey makes a choice to stay in the adventure. This could be interpreted as Rey seeing BB8 as a child figure whom she needs to take care of, in the way that Dorothy sees Toto in *The Wizard of Oz*. However, there is nothing in the film that gives this impression. As a heroine, why would she stay? As a hero, of course she would stay; she has to save the galaxy and find Luke Skywalker.

Rey and BB8 go down a flight of stairs leading to the basement. Rey hears voices but does not know where they are coming from. A door automatically opens, and Rey enters a musty room filled with old relics. She is drawn toward a small chest, which she opens to find a lightsaber. The minute she touches it, things change. She "sees" scenes from her own past that she was involved in, then she sees Luke's past, and finally, her future, then she comes back to the dusty room in the basement. She looks up to see Maz Kanata, who tells her the lightsaber in the chest was Luke's, and his fathers before him. Now it calls to her. Rey tells Maz that she must go back to Jakku. Maz tells her that whoever she is waiting for is not coming back. "The belonging you seek is not behind you but ahead. . . . Find Luke." This could be a hero's Call to Destiny or, unbeknownst to the audience, a heroine's call to help family. Maz tells Rey to take the lightsaber. Rey resists and runs out of the castle and into the forest. The lightsaber is a hero's weapon, not a heroine's weapon. The female's symbolic weapons are long-distance weapons, such as Wonder Woman's lasso and Katniss's bow. At this point, Rey is still following the hero's journey, not the heroine's journey. However, the darkness of the forest is the female's domain.

The First Order (the bad guys) have a big ceremony and announce a weapon that will destroy the Republic, which they then proceed to shoot. This is reminiscent of the Death Star destroying Leia's home planet in Episode IV. Han and Finn see the weapon's red streaks of fire in the sky, and Finn asks where Rey is. They then see the TIE fighters in the sky, which start shooting. The destruction of Maz Kanata's castle begins. Rey also sees the fighters and realizes they are after BB8. This realization can be interpreted as Rey's heroine instincts wanting to protect BB8. She runs back toward the castle. Maz shows Finn and Han the lightsaber that belonged to Luke.

TIE fighters destroy the castle, and stormtroopers on the ground shoot everyone. The Rebel Resistance (the good guys) fly to the rescue in their X-wing fighters. In the forest, Rey meets Kylo Ren, who uses the Force on her and takes her hostage. Finn and Han see Kylo Ren taking Rey into his plane with him. The main ship from the Resistance lands, and C-3PO and General Leia emerge. There is a reunion. Back at the Resistance base, Finn and Poe also reunite. BB8 finds R2-D2, who has been unresponsive since Luke left.

Rey is in chains in a chair. Kylo Ren is in the room, and he takes his helmet/mask off for the first time. Using the Force, he gets inside Rey's head to try to find where the Resistance base is located, but she does not crack. Then she gets inside Kylo Ren's head, and he realizes she has the Force within her. Later, Kylo Ren tells Snoke (the main bad guy) that the Force is strong in Rey but that she has had no training. Snoke wants to see her.

Rey is still in chains in the chair. She uses the power of the Force on the stormtrooper who is guarding her and gets him to take the chains off of her. It takes her three attempts, but she does it. This is reminiscent of Obi-Wan Kenobi telling the stormtroopers to "move along, these aren't the droids you're looking for" in Episode IV. Kylo Ren comes back to find her gone, and he has a temper tantrum.

Back at the Resistance base, the resistance fighters make plans to blow up the new weapon. This is reminiscent of the plans to blow up the Death Star in Episode IV.

Han, Chewie, and Finn leave for the First Order planet. Kylo Ren is looking for Rey but suddenly feels Han's presence. X-wing fighters begin their attack. Rey meets back up with everyone, and they plan their escape. Realizing the rebels in the X-wings are not winning the battle, they go back to plant explosives instead of leaving. Han finds Kylo Ren and wants him to come home (Kylo Ren is Leia and Han's son) and get away from Snoke and the dark side. Kylo Ren kills Han. Chewie detonates the reactors, and Finn and Rey run to get back to the Millennium Falcon before the planet blows up.

Kylo Ren meets Finn and Rey in the snowy forest as they try to escape. Kylo Ren and Finn battle with lightsabers.

Finn loses, and he drops Luke's lightsaber. Kylo Ren tries to draw it to him, but the lightsaber goes into Rey's hands instead. She activates it and fights Kylo Ren, winning the fight. The Millennium Falcon shows up with Chewbacca flying it. They carry Finn onboard and head back to the Resistance base just as the planet explodes. Once they land, Leia and Rey hug, Chewie gets tended to, Finn is still unconscious, and R2-D2 wakes up and gives everyone the information they are looking for to find Luke.

Rey and Chewbacca fly off to find him. They land on an island where the original Jedi Temple is. Rey climbs the mountain to the top of the island and hands Luke his lightsaber.

This story is a hero's journey, not a heroine's journey, although there are a few symbolic feminine moments. Rey has no heroine's reason to take this journey unless BB8 is viewed as representing her family. But the film doesn't continue this relationship; BB8 belongs to Poe, the pilot. A hero taking this journey would do exactly what Rey does in the film. The plot too closely follows Episode IV, in which Luke was beginning his journey as a hero. This film is Luke Skywalker's story retold with a female playing Luke's part.

Rey uses no feminine characteristics or symbolism to accomplish her goals. In fact, she has no real reason to be doing what she does. Family is not in trouble, she is not in a transformative time in her life, nor is she integrating. Rey just goes from scene to scene, reacting to whatever is put in front of her. She does not have a mentor, ruthless or kind, unless Maz Kanata survives and becomes one in a future episode. BB8 is Rey's sidekick for a short time, but the droid actually belongs to someone else and is too childlike to be her mentor or protect her. One feminine attribute is Rey's attraction to Finn, but she doesn't stand by him on any occasion. Some of what she does would have been more satisfying and psychologically believable if she were trying to save him, such as Katniss doing what is needed to save Peeta when he is hurt in *The Hunger Games*.

Rey is a character that can do no wrong. Even though Luke is the chosen one just as Rey is, he has faults, and he grows and learns. Rey knows everything without instruction or mentoring. She has no faults; she is too perfect. An audience falls in love with someone who tries, fails, and keeps on trying, as these human traits are relatable. Rey never fails at anything she attempts. She can not only fly the Millennium Falcon effortlessly, but she can fix it, too. As Valerie Estelle Frankel observes, Rey uses the Force to have the guard release her even though she has had no instruction in the Force. Also, it takes her only three tries. Just hours before this, Rey had never heard of the Force. With a lightsaber she has never used before, she fights Kylo Ren, who has trained for many years, and defeats him without getting a scratch on her. This story is the journey of a hero, not a heroine.

Feminine Heroic Themes

Let's now look at these films as a collective. Were there themes that ran through all of the journeys that you can use when creating your films? What was missing that you might want to include? Let's dig in and see if we can find some themes that will help you going forward.

The common theme of the specific journey for each heroine is that she can take her journey for more than one reason. You don't have to stick with transformation or saving family specifically. In *Beauty and the Beast*, Belle takes a journey of transformation from maiden to woman, but she is also saving her family in the form of her father and the Beast. In *The Wizard of Oz*, Dorothy sets out to save her little dog, Toto, and finds herself on a journey of transformation from girl to woman. This journey is not a sexual transformation but one of knowledgeable empowerment. *Moana* sets out on her journey to help save her village but validates the voice inside her telling her to go to the ocean, listening to her intuition. This is the journey of integration. In *Star Wars*, Rey takes an adventure because of destiny. She is the only heroine who takes Campbell's classic journey of the hero.

In looking for the types of mentors for the heroine, sadly, we see that none of the films use the symbolic sisters. Disney took out the symbolic sister's role in its adaptation of *Beauty and the Beast*, which I interpret as a masculine bias. The other films didn't include sisters in the storyline at all, although one could possibly interpret Dorothy's buddies as metaphorical sisters. Moana was left to figure life out on her own.

Dorothy is the only heroine to have both a fairy godmother and a dark mother mentor. Glinda the Good Witch of the North helps her along the Yellow Brick Road, and the Wicked Witch of the West pushes her to recognize her own power. In the original written version of this tale, the Wicked Witch's role is bigger, and she pushes Dorothy even further. *Moana* has the fairy godmother symbolism in the form of Gramma giving Moana pep talks, telling her forbidden stories, and encouraging her to listen to her own calling and to go to the ocean. There is no dark mother for Moana, but she does see both dark and light in the forms of Ta Kā and Te Fiti. However, neither were her mentors, and Belle has no mentors at all. No sisters, no fairy godmother or dark evil witch. This doesn't sit right with the feminine psyche. We feel as if something is missing or just not quite believable. Every heroine needs mentors. Remember to put them in your stories.

As discussed in earlier chapters, the use of small animals in traditional female tales symbolizes the instinctive function or intuition for the heroine. None of the four films include small animals that specifically perform this function. In *Moana*, the heroine has her little pig and her chicken, but they do not symbolically represent Moana's intuition. They do not help or guide her in any way during her journey. However, she does have the ocean, which helps her. After the storm, the ocean washes her up on the island where Maui lives, and when Maui wants to be rid of her, the ocean keeps bringing her back to him. The ocean also parts for Moana so Ta Kā can come toward her. Disney did a good job casting the ocean as Moana's feminine mentor.

There are no small animals in *The Wizard of Oz*; instead, Scarecrow, Tin Man, and the Cowardly Lion are used. These characters function psychologically as Dorothy's instincts. It is unusual to use masculine mentors in a heroine's journey, but these characters work perfectly. They want the attributes that Dorothy herself wants. She thinks she must look outside herself for them and have them given to her when, in reality, she has had them all along. BB8 is Rey's temporary mentor in *Star Wars Episode VII*. Symbolically, the little droid is Rey's intuitive side at the beginning of the film. She intuitively decides not to sell the droid, and she accepts its advice about Finn. However, throughout the rest of the film, BB8 does not fill this role for Rey.

The questionable film for symbolism of the heroine's instinct is *Beauty and the Beast*. Belle has the talking furniture, but they are not symbolically her intuition. One might consider some of them, such as Mrs. Potts and the wardrobe, as guiding female figures, but I think this is a stretch because the audience knows from the beginning that they are human staff of the castle. The original tale does not include small animals, but it does include sister mentorship.

Three of the four heroines in these films do not use any type of violence to complete their journeys. Moana does not use violence to restore the heart of Ta Kā. In *Beauty and the Beast*, there is violence between Gaston and the Beast, and the household items proclaim war on the villagers who come looking for the Beast, but Belle herself does not use violence at any time. In the original written tale, there is no violence anywhere in the story. The violence in this film is all Disney's creation.

In *The Wizard of Oz*, Scarecrow is lit on fire. Dorothy does what is needed to save him by throwing water on him, and inadvertently melts the Wicked Witch. She does not take possession of the Wicked Witch's broom by violence but by saving her friend. The only film in which the heroine is violent is *Star Wars: Episode VII*. Rey uses a lightsaber to try to kill Kylo Ren. This would be expected in a hero's journey, not a heroine's journey.

Another profoundly feminine attribute we have discussed

is the metaphorical deep sleep. The only film that includes this is *The Wizard of Oz*, when Dorothy gets knocked on the head by the window shutter during the storm. This time of unconsciousness symbolically allows for her transformation. None of the other films have this symbolism.

The heroine, Rey, in *Star Wars: Episode VII* is taking the masculine heroic journey. However, and surprisingly, there are moments that give us hope that Disney may change the storyline in future episodes to bring in more feminine symbolism that will have Rey taking a heroine's journey. The first sign of hope is the feminine nature of BB8. Another is the character of Maz Kanata, who could easily become Rey's female mentor or fairy godmother in future episodes. Rey shows the feminine trait of patience as she waits for her family to come back to Jakku. She also declines Han Solo's job offer because she needs to go home and wait for her family. This is a classic heroine's journey.

These analyses show that films can portray the heroine's journey in many creative forms. These films represent the type of journeys the heroine can take: the journey to help and reunite family, the journey of transformation from maiden to mother to crone, and finally, the psychological integration that transformation can bring. They demonstrate that the heroine has no need for violence to achieve her heroic deeds, and she has feminine-oriented mentors that teach, guide, and support her. Disappointingly, none of the films included in their storylines two important factors: the importance of the symbolic sisters and the marriage initiation. After viewing many hours of female-oriented films, I believe these important symbols are either being discarded by filmmakers or they do not know the importance of the symbols.

As you have seen through the analysis of these four films and from the discussions throughout this book, you can make films that have focus on the heroine and include the symbolism that is exclusively hers. Using the guiding principles of the *The Heroine's Journey for Filmmakers,* you can give Old Joe the boot and *finally* create female characters that females can relate to!

Acknowledgments

As all authors and filmmakers know, there is a plethora of people that stand behind you to get the job done. This book is no different. I'd like to acknowledge a few of my heroes and heroines that helped with this book as well as supporting me through life.

The first and most important is my brother, Bruce Ross. He was my first hero and continues to be my hero. He has never faltered in his support of me. There are no words that can express my gratitude and love.

I cannot say enough about my thesis team from SOU. Kristin Nagy-Catz you pushed me, and I needed it. Brook Colley you met me where I was and I'm so grateful for that. Erik Palmer you trusted me and believed in me when I didn't.

To my editor Jessica Vineyard, how lucky am I to call you a friend as well as my professional guru. You made magic happen at times. So Grateful.

To the team at TheAuthorIncubator.com, thank you for believing in the authors you support.

Big Hugs of gratitude to Christy Collins at Constellation Book Services. An amazing lady with amazing design talent.

To everyone at The Oak Tree, thank you for the back booth and the Bloody Mary's and bacon. Gary, Sammy, Dolce and all my other buddies, you were my support team and still are.

To the many heroines that I have the privilege of calling friends, I hold deep gratitude for each and every one of you. Below are just a few of the many that have crossed my path:

Pat Erramouspe, you have always been more than a friend to me. My original soul sister. We have history girl.

Marlise Cromar, you always set me straight right when I need it the most. Plus, you love an adventure as much as I do!

Trish Withus, you are my angel. Whereas I'm still an angel in training.

Lupe Simms, my academic heroine. You reminded me of my past and what I can now do with my future.

Donna Walters, once again there are no words for the support you have given me. Plus, being my bubbly drinking BFF.

And no heroine is complete without her fairy godmother. I was blessed to have three when I was growing up and I lost them much too soon. Mom, Grandma and Michele, this book could have never been written without the love and guidance I received from each of you. You are the good that I try to encapsulate in my life each and every day.

If you'd like to connect with me,
I'd love to hear from you.
heroinesforfilm@gmail.com